A Year's Worth of Gospel Acclamations

Sundays, Weekdays, Solemnities, Saints, Mary,
Christian Initiation, Penance, Marriage, Funerals

HANDBOOK

*A liturgical service takes on a nobler aspect
when the rites are celebrated with singing…*

Constitution on the Sacred Liturgy, 113.

© The Theology Forum
The Cloyne Commission for Liturgical Formation

Acknowledgements

Most Gospel acclamation verses herein are from the New Revised Standard Version of the Bible, copyrighted 1989 the Division of Christian Education of the National Council of the Churches of Christ in the United States of America, and are used by permission. All rights reserved.
Remaining Gospel acclamation verses are excerpts from the English translation of *The Roman Missal* © 1973, International Committee on English in the Liturgy, Inc. All rights reserved.
Most texts in Irish are from *Leabhar Aifrinn An Domhnaigh*, An tAthair Pádraig Ó Fiannachta, Gaeltarra Éireann na Forbacha, Gaillimh, © 1978.

Excerpt from: "The Constitution on the Sacred Liturgy". The Liturgy Documents - volume one, third edition, Elizabeth Hoffman, ed. Chicago: LTP, 1991.

Copyright: Aifreann II: Gospel Acclamation, Bernard Sexton, © 1996; Aifreann Eoin na Croise: Gospel Acclamation, Peadar Ó Riada, © Realworld Music 1993; Mass For The People: Gospel Acclamation, Mary Pedder Daly, © 2006; Mass Of Creation: Gospel Acclamation, Marty Haugen, © 1984, GIA Publications, Inc; Mass Of God's Promise: Gospel Acclamation, Daniel L. Schutte, © 1996, OCP Publications. All rights reserved; Mass Of Light: Gospel Acclamation, David Haas, © 1988, GIA Publications, Inc; Mass Of Peace: Gospel Acclamation, Seóirse Bodley, © 1976; Mass Of Saint Finbarr: Gospel Acclamation, Patrick Killeen, © 2004, Upbeat Publications; Mass Of Saint John Of The Cross: Gospel Acclamation, Ronan McDonagh, © 1991; Mass Of The Annunciation: Gospel Acclamation, Fintan O' Carroll, © 1982, O' Carroll Publications. All rights reserved; Psalm 117: Easter Alleluia: Tone, Anthony Milner (A.M.), © 1972, Mayhew / McCrimmon Ltd.; Psalm 117: Easter Alleluia: Tone, Margaret Daly (M.D.D.), © 1992, Veritas Publications; Paschal Mass - based on 'O filii et filiae': Gospel Acclamation, acc. by Richard Proulx, © 1975, 2000, GIA Publications, Inc; Roman Missal - Mode VI: Gospel Acclamation, Plainsong; Sacred Story – A Celtic Celebration: Gospel Acclamation, Liam Lawton, © 1996, Maelruain Publications, Saint Mary's Priory, Tallaght, Dublin 24, Ireland; Saint Benedict's Centenary Mass: Gospel Acclamation, Margaret Daly, © 1980, Irish Institute of Pastoral Liturgy; Alleluia - Magnificat: Gospel Acclamation, John Paul Lécot / Paul Décha © 2001, Édition Lethielleux – repertoire Multilingue Nouvelle Édition.
Additional verse tones © Dominic Finn (D.F.) and © Mary Mc Sweeney (M. Mc S.) used with permission.

Diocesan Director for Liturgical Music: Fr. Gerard Coleman

Special thanks to:
Sr. Emmanuel Leonard, Moya Muldowney
Sr. Moira Bergin, Fr Patrick Jones of the National Centre for Liturgy, Saint Patrick's College, Maynooth
Council Members of the Irish Church Music Association
Eileen Greaney, Fr. James Killeen of the Cloyne Diocesan Centre, Cobh
Most Rev. John Magee DD, Bishop of Cloyne

The Artwork: Cover - oil pastel on rag paper; inside cover - watercolour resist on rag paper. Rita Scannell
Photographs on pages 5, 6 & 8 by Richard Mills birdpics@newsguy.com

Prepared by the Committee for Liturgical Music
Music Editors: Dominic Finn, Tim Fouhy, Carmel O' Shea
General Editor and Design: Rita Scannell – ritascannelldesign@eircom.net
Printed by Collins Print in Cork, Ireland – www.collinsprint.ie

Introduction

A Year's Worth of Gospel Acclamations has three elements: A leader's handbook, a leader's box-set of two CDs and a musician's accompaniment edition. When a liturgically-formed cantor, choir or musician is unavailable to lead the Gospel acclamation of the day, another person can be trained to carry out the role, using this resource as a start-up kit. He/she would sing from their place in the congregation.

The principles underlying this resource are, namely:

- A single Gospel acclamation text can be used on most days of a liturgical season, instead of using the text of the day.
- One musical setting is used for an entire liturgical season. While two / three settings are given for most seasons, one setting is chosen. It is used exclusively throughout the particular season. When the liturgical season changes, a different selection of musical settings is provided. Again, select and use only one throughout (see page 204)!
- You must know the particular liturgical day being celebrated and which liturgical season it is. You must also know if texts specific to marriage and funerals, for example, can be used on this day. *The Liturgical Calendar for Ireland* tells you which liturgical day and season it is and if marriage and funerals texts, etc., are permitted.

How to use *A Year's Worth of Gospel Acclamations*:

1. Consult the *Liturgical Calendar for Ireland* and confer with the presider.
2. Having identified the liturgical season, day, and celebration, go to the Index for the Seasons of the Liturgical Year of this handbook (pages 9 - 23). Here, in the section for the relevant season, you are directed to a designated text according to your musical setting. Open this page. Note the CD information.
3. Listen to the track and, if necessary, a track of the same Mass setting that includes the refrain. Practice aloud the refrain, refrain, verse, refrain sequence.

In Church, lead a Gospel acclamation as follows:
As leader, sing the Alleluia (or Lenten) refrain. If available, use a mobile microphone – be careful not to shout! The assembly repeats this refrain. You, alone, sing the two-line verse. The assembly repeats the refrain.

For more information on how to conduct the Liturgy of the Word correctly, see:
The Word of the Lord and *The Ministry of the Word – A Compilation of Sources*.
These books are published by the Cloyne Commission for Liturgical Formation.

Committee for Liturgical Music:
Fr. Gerard Coleman, Dominic Finn, Carmel Gleeson, Sr. Emmanuel Leonard, Mary Mc Sweeney, Fr Jeremiah O' Riordan, Mary Pedder-Daly, Mairéad Shannon.

The Word of the Lord
A book for forming all ministers of the word; this is the most up-to-date, accurate and accessible resource for conducting the Liturgy of the Word. It is a 'How To' book!

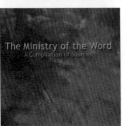

The Ministry of the Word – A Compilation of Sources
A companion to *The Word of the Lord*; this is a reference book for primary sources, further explanation and sample intentions for the Prayer of the Faithful. It is a 'Why' book!

A Year's Worth of Gospel Acclamations: CD
Sundays, Weekdays, Solemnities, Saints, Mary,
Christian Initiation, Penance, Marriage, Funerals

A practical aid, especially for new cantors; this double CD pack will enable the singing of the Gospel acclamation in all celebrations of the Liturgy with a congregation.

A Year's Worth of Gospel Acclamations: HANDBOOK
Sundays, Weekdays, Solemnities, Saints, Mary,
Christian Initiation, Penance, Marriage, Funerals
An easy to use manual of Gospel acclamation texts and music; this should be used in conjunction with the annual *Liturgical Calendar for Ireland*.

COMING SOON..................

A Year's Worth of Gospel Acclamations: ACCOMPANIMENT
Sundays, Weekdays, Solemnities, Saints, Mary,
Christian Initiation, Penance, Marriage, Funerals
Third in the Gospel acclamation series; it is aimed at musicians.

Available from:
Publications, Cloyne Diocesan Centre, Cobh, Co. Cork
Tel: 021-481 1430   Fax: 021-481 1026   Email: cloyne@indigo.ie
And from Veritas nationwide www.veritas.ie

A Year's Worth of Gospel Acclamations is a resource to help parishes meet the requirement of liturgical law, namely:
(1) The Alleluia or verse before the Gospel must be sung. *General Introduction to the Lectionary*, 23;
(2) An acclamation of this kind constitutes a rite or act in itself, by which the assembly of the faithful welcomes and greets the Lord who is about to speak to it in the Gospel and professes their faith by means of the chant. It is sung by all while standing and is led by the choir or a cantor (…). The verse, however, is sung either by the choir or by the cantor. *General Instruction of the Roman Missal*, 2002, 62.

Given this obligation to sing rather than merely recite the Gospel acclamation, especially in celebrations of the Liturgy with a congregation, I warmly welcome *A Year's Worth of Gospel Acclamations* – as a tuition handbook, accompanying CD and instrumental edition. I trust it will prove itself an accessible, practical and enriching support where pastors and parishioners collaborate for an authentic and more fruitful celebration of the Church's Liturgy.

It is with deep gratitude that I recommend this latest resource of the Cloyne Commission for Liturgical Formation. Using it, may you have cause for gratitude too: the liturgical assembly newly at ease with its song and so greeting the Lord Jesus with a more wholehearted expression of faith!

+ John Magee

Bishop of Cloyne
Chairperson of the Irish Episcopal Commission for Liturgy

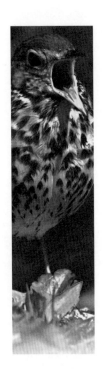

Contents

Praise the Lord!
Praise the name of the Lord;
give praise, O servants of the Lord.

Psalm 135

INDEX

for the
Seasons of the Liturgical Year

The Season of Advent   **Turn to Page**

The Season of Advent

Turn to Page (s)

Rite of Baptism for Children
On the 1st, 2nd, 3rd, 4th Sundays of Advent (Outside Mass)   24 or 27

Rite of Penance
On the Weekdays of the 1st, 2nd, 3rd Weeks of Advent   24 or 27 or 29
On the Weekdays 17th - 23rd of December   26 or 29

Rite of Marriage
On the Weekdays of the 1st, 2nd, 3rd Weeks of Advent   154 to 158
On the Weekdays 17th - 24th of December   154 to 158

Order of Funerals ✱
On the 1st, 2nd, 3rd, 4th Sundays of Advent   ☒   24 or 27
On the Immaculate Conception   ☒   24 or 27

On the Weekdays of the 1st, 2nd, 3rd Weeks of Advent   161 or 166 to 174
On the Weekdays 17th - 23rd of December   161 or 166 to 174
On the Weekday of the 24th of December   ●   161 or 166 to 174

Christmas Eve Reception of the Body at the Church before the Vigil Mass   26 or 29

Anniversary Masses for the Dead
on the 17th - 24th of December   26 or 29

● = Excluding the Reception of the Body at the Church on Christmas Eve
☒ = Funeral Mass Texts are not permitted today.
✱ = 'Order of Funerals' includes the Reception of the Body at the Church.

The Season of Christmas

(NR) = Not Recorded.

⬤ = excluding the Reception of the Body at the Church on evening of January 5th.
☒ = Funeral Mass Texts are not permitted today.
◻ = Anniversary Masses for the Dead Texts are not permitted on this day.
(NR) = Not Recorded.
✱ = Order of Funerals' includes the Reception of the Body at the Church.

Ordinary Time after Christmas

◻ = Anniversary Masses for the Dead Texts are not permitted on this day.

✱ = 'Order of Funerals' includes the Reception of the Body at the Church.

The Season of Lent

◻ = Anniversary Masses for the Dead Texts are not permitted on this day.

(NR) = Not Recorded.

The Season of Lent

Turn to Page (s)

Rite of Christian Initiation of Adults

The Rite of Election   57 or 183 A (NR)

The Rite of Penance

On Ash Wednesday   159

On the Thursday, Friday, Saturday after Ash Wednesday   159

On the Monday to Saturday of the 1st, 2nd, 3rd, 4th, 5th Weeks of Lent   159

On the Monday, Tuesday, Wednesday in Holy Week   65

Order of Funerals ✶

On Ash Wednesday   ◻   164 or 166 to 174

On the Thursday, Friday, Saturday after Ash Wednesday   164 or 166 to 174

On the 1st Sunday of Lent   ☒   57 or 183 A (NR)

On the 2nd Sunday of Lent   ☒   57 or 183 B (NR)

On the 3rd Sunday of Lent   ☒   57 or 183 C (NR)

On the 4th Sunday of Lent   ☒   57 or 183 D (NR)

On the 5th Sunday of Lent   ☒   58 or 183 E (NR)

On Palm Sunday of the Lord's Passion   ☒   64

On the Monday to Saturday of the 1st, 2nd, 3rd, 4th, 5th Weeks of Lent   164 or 166 to 174

On Monday, Tuesday, Wednesday in Holy Week   ◻   165 or 166 to 174

On the Feast of the Chair of Saint Peter, Apostle   ◻   164 or 166 to 174

On the Solemnity of Saint Patrick   ●   ☒   ◻   59 or 60

Reception of the Body at the Church on the evening of March 16th   59 or 60

On the Solemnity of Saint Joseph   ◻   164 or 166 to 174

On the Solemnity of the Annunciation of the Lord   ◻   164 or 166 to 174

● = including the Reception of the Body at the Church on the evening of March 16th

☒ = Funeral Mass Texts are not permitted today.

◻ = Anniversary Masses for the Dead Texts are not permitted on this day.

(NR) = Not Recorded.

✶ = 'Order of Funerals' includes the Reception of the Body at the Church.

The Easter Triduum

Turn to Page

The Easter Triduum

Turn to Page (s)

◈ = A Funeral Mass is not celebrated today. A Liturgy of the Word is celebrated, instead.
● = excluding the Reception of the Body at the Church on Holy Saturday evening.
☒ = Funeral Mass Texts are not permitted today.
◻ = Anniversary Masses for the Dead Texts are not permitted on this day.
✳ = 'Order of Funerals' includes the Reception of the Body at the Church (Note: ●).

The Season of Easter

Turn to Page (s)

Sundays

Weekdays

Weekday Solemnity

Weekday Feasts

○ = Instead of Mass Of Saint Finbarr, Mass Of The Annunciation, or Mass Of Saint John Of The Cross, use the refrain and verse tone of Paschal Mass, Mass Of God's Promise or Mode VI for the acclamation texts on pages 113 - 115 or 122 - 124, as applies.
(NR) = Not Recorded.

The Season of Easter

● = Instead of Mass Of Saint Finbarr, Mass Of The Annunciation, or Mass Of Saint John Of The Cross, use the refrain and verse tone of Paschal Mass, Mass Of God's Promise or Mode VI for the acclamation texts on pages 113 - 115 or 122 - 124, as applies.

☒ = Funeral Mass Texts are not permitted today.

◻ = Anniversary Masses for the Dead Texts are not permitted on this day.

(NR) = Not Recorded.

✶ = 'Order of Funerals' includes the Reception of the Body at the Church.

⊗ = Baptism, Confirmation, First Eucharist.

Ordinary Time after the Season of Easter

† = Use the refrain and verse tone of Mass Of Saint Finbarr, Mass Of The Annunciation, or Mass Of Saint John Of The Cross.

◻ = Anniversary Masses for the Dead Texts are not permitted on this day.

(NR) = Not Recorded.

Ordinary Time after the Season of Easter

Rite of Baptism for Children (Outside Mass)

On the Solemnity of the Most Holy Trinity — 106 or 107 or 108

On the Solemnity of the Body and Blood of Christ — 109 or 110 or 111

On all Sundays after the Solemnity of the Body and Blood of Christ up until and
including the 33rd Sunday in Ordinary Time, but excluding, 1 - 5 following: — 82 to 85

1 The Solemnity of the Birth of Saint John the Baptist, — 116 or 117 or 118

2 The Solemnity of Saints Peter and Paul, Apostles, — 119 or 120 or 121

3 The Solemnity of the Assumption of the Blessed Virgin Mary — 126 to 131

4 The Solemnity of All Saints — 139 or 140 or 141

5 The Commemoration of all the Faithful Departed

On the Solemnity of Our Lord Jesus Christ, Universal King — 151 or 152 or 153

The Rite of Penance

On all weekdays in Ordinary Time after the Season of Easter excluding: — 160

1 The Solemnity of the Birth of Saint John the Baptist, ⊙

2 The Solemnity of Saints Peter and Paul, Apostles, ⊙

3 The Solemnity of the Assumption of the Virgin Mary ⊙

4 The Solemnity of All Saints ⊙

5 The Commemoration of all the Faithful Departed ⊙

The Rite of Marriage

On all weekdays in Ordinary Time after the Season of Easter excluding: — 154 to 158

1 The Solemnity of the Birth of Saint John the Baptist, ⊙ — 116 or 117 or 118

2 The Solemnity of Saints Peter and Paul, Apostles, ⊙ — 119 or 120 or 121

3 The Solemnity of the Assumption of the Virgin Mary ⊙ — 126 to 131

4 The Solemnity of All Saints ⊙ — 139 or 140 or 141

5 The Commemoration of all the Faithful Departed ⊙ — 142 or 143 or 144

Order of Funerals✶

On the Solemnity of the Most Holy Trinity — 106 or 107 or 108

On the Solemnity of the Body and Blood of Christ — 109 or 110 or 111

On all Sundays after the Solemnity of the Body and Blood of Christ up until and
including the 33rd Sunday in Ordinary Time — 166 to 174

On the Solemnity of Our Lord Jesus Christ, Universal King — 151 or 152 or 153

On all weekdays in Ordinary Time after the Season of Easter excluding: — 166 to 174

The Solemnity of the Assumption of the Virgin Mary ◻ — 126 to 131

The Solemnity of All Saints ◻ — 139 or 140 or 141

The Commemoration of all the Faithful Departed ◻ — 142 or 143 or 144

⊙ = When these Solemnities occur on a weekday.

◻ = Anniversary Masses for the Dead Texts are not permitted.

✶ = 'Order of Funerals' includes the Reception of the Body at the Church.

Advent

Alleluia - Magnificat

CD 1 / Track 2

Lécot / Décha

Al - le - lu - ia, al - le - lu - ia, al - le - lu - ia!

M. Mc S.

Look, the Lord will come to save his people.

Blessed those who are ready to meet him.

Alleluia - Magnificat

CD 1 / Track 3

Lécot / Décha

Al - le - lu - ia, al - le - lu - ia, al - le - lu - ia!

M. Mc S.

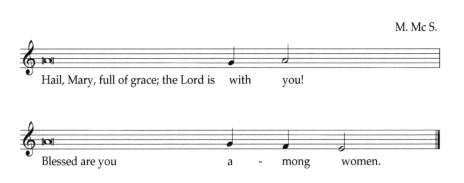

Hail, Mary, full of grace; the Lord is with you!

Blessed are you a - mong women.

Alleluia - Magnificat

CD 1 / Track 4

Lécot / Décha

Al - le - lu - ia, al - le - lu - ia, al - le - lu - ia!

M. Mc S.

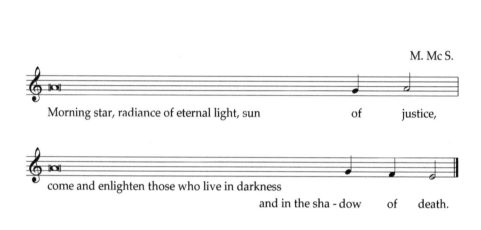

Morning star, radiance of eternal light, sun   of   justice,

come and enlighten those who live in darkness

and in the sha - dow   of   death.

Advent

Mass For The People

CD 1 / Track 5

Mary Pedder Daly

Al - le - lu - ia, al - le - lu - ia, al - le - lu - u - ia.

al - le - lu - ia, al - le - lu - ia, al - le - lu_____ ia.

Prepare the way of the Lord, make his paths straight.

And all flesh shall see the salva - tion of God.

Advent

CD 1 / Track 6

Mass For The People

Mary Pedder Daly

Al - le - lu - ia,   al - le - lu - ia,   al - le - lu - u - ia.

al - le - lu - ia,   al - le - lu - ia,   al - le - lu____ ia.

Hail Mary, full of grace; the Lord is with you!

Blessed are you   a - mong   women.

Mass For The People

CD 1 / Track 7

Mary Pedder Daly

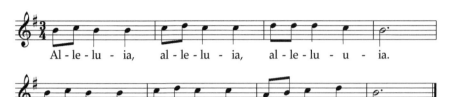

Al - le - lu - ia,   al - le - lu - ia,   al - le - lu - u - ia.

al - le - lu - ia,   al - le - lu - ia,   al - le - lu____ ia.

Wisdom of the Most High, ordering all things with strength and gentleness,

come and teach us the   way   of   truth.

Mass Of Peace

Seóirse Bodley

CD 1 / Track 8

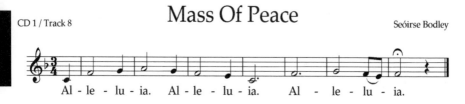

Al - le - lu - ia. Al - le - lu - ia. Al - le - lu - ia.

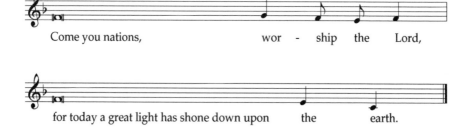

Come you nations, wor - ship the Lord,

for today a great light has shone down upon the earth.

Mass Of Peace

CD 1 / Track 9

Seóirse Bodley

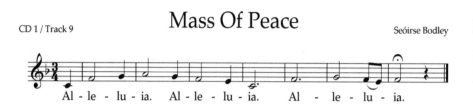

Al - le - lu - ia. Al - le - lu - ia. Al - le - lu - ia.

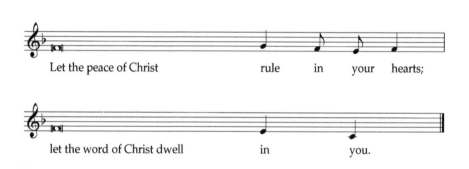

Let the peace of Christ   rule   in   your   hearts;

let the word of Christ dwell   in   you.

CD 1 / Track 10

Mass Of Peace

Seóirse Bodley

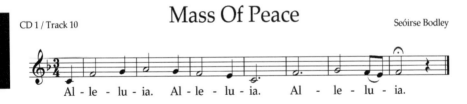

Al - le - lu - ia.   Al - le - lu - ia.   Al - le - lu - ia.

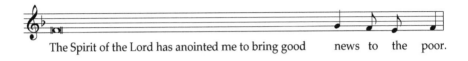

The Spirit of the Lord has anointed me to bring good   news to the poor.

He has sent me to proclaim release   to   captives.

Mass Of Peace

CD 1 / Track 11

Seóirse Bodley

Christmas

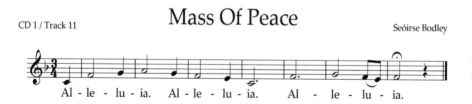

Al - le - lu - ia. Al - le - lu - ia. Al - le - lu - ia.

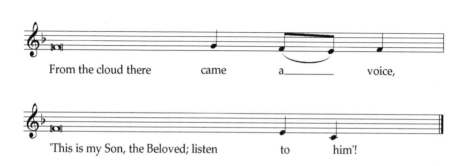

From the cloud there came a_____ voice,

'This is my Son, the Beloved; listen to him'!

Mass Of Light

CD 1 / Track 12

David Haas

Al - le - lu - ia. al - le - lu - ia, al - le - lu - ia.

Al-le - lu - ia, al - le - lu - ia, al - le - lu ia.

D. F.

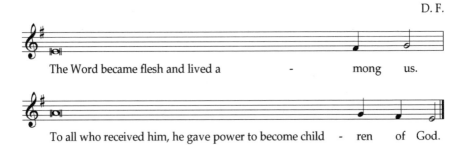

The Word became flesh and lived a - mong us.

To all who received him, he gave power to become child - ren of God.

Mass Of Light

CD 1 / Track 13

David Haas

Al - le - lu - ia. al - le - lu - ia, al - le - lu - ia.

Al - le - lu - ia, al - le - lu - ia, al - le - lu____ ia.

D.F.

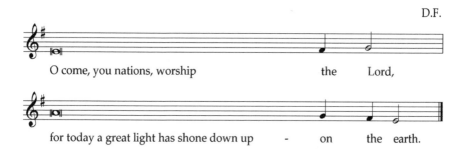

O come, you nations, worship the Lord,

for today a great light has shone down up - on the earth.

Mass Of Light

CD 1 / Track 14

David Haas

Christmas

Al - le - lu - ia.   al - le - lu - ia,   al - le - lu - ia.

Al - le - lu - ia,   al - le - lu - ia,   al - le - lu ia.

D. F.

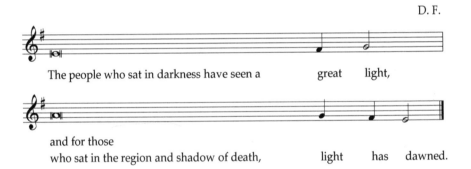

The people who sat in darkness have seen a   great   light,

and for those
who sat in the region and shadow of death,   light   has   dawned.

Mass Of Light

CD 1 / Track 15

David Haas

Al - le - lu - ia.   al - le - lu - ia,   al - le - lu - ia.

Al - le - lu - ia,   al - le - lu - ia,   al - le - lu - ia.

D. F.

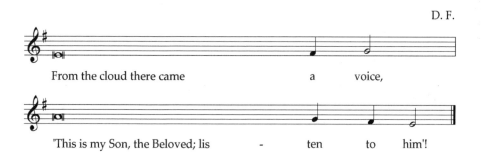

From the cloud there came   a   voice,

'This is my Son, the Beloved; lis - ten   to   him'!

37

Aifreann II

CD 1 / Track 16

Bernard Sexton

Al - le - lu - ia, al - le - lu - ia, Al - le - lú - ia.

Al - le - lu - ia, al - le - lu - ia, al - le - lú - ia.

D.F.

'Is mise solas an t-saoil' a   deir an   Tiarna;

'an té a leanfaidh mise, beidh aige   so-las na   beatha'.

Aifreann II

CD 1 / Track 17

Bernard Sexton

Al - le -lu- ia, al - le-lu - ia, Al - le - lu - ia.

Al - le-lu - ia, al - le-lu - ia, al - le-lu - ia.

D.F.

Is tú Peadar, agus is ar an gcarraig seo a thógfaidh mé____ m'Eaglais,

agus ní bhuafaidh geataí i - frinn uirthi.

Aifreann II

CD 1 / Track 18

Bernard Sexton

Al - le - lu - ia, al - le - lu - ia, Al - le - lu - ia.

Al - le - lu - ia, al - le - lu - ia, al - le - lu - ia.

D.F.

Rinne mé sibh a thogagh,
agus a cheapadh chun go n-imeodh sibh agus to-radh a thabhairt

agus go mairfead bhur___ dtoradh.

40

Aifreann II

CD 1 / Track 19

Bernard Sexton

Al – le - lu – ia, al – le - lu – ia, Al – le - lu – ia.

Al – le - lu - ia, al – le - lu – ia, al – le - lu – ia.

D.F.

Tar, a   chéi - le   Chríost;

glac an chóroin atá ullamh ag Críost duit ón tsío – raí-ocht i   leith.

Aifreann II

CD 1 / Track 20

Bernard Sexton

Al - le - lu - ia, al - le - lu - ia, Al - le - lu - ia.

Al - le - lu - ia, al - le - lu - ia, al - le - lu - ia.

D.F.

Solas chun na náisiúin a shoil - siú

agus glóir do phobail, Is - rá - él.

42

Aifreann II

CD 1 / Track 21

Bernard Sexton

Al - le - lu - ia, al - le - lu - ia, Al - le - lú - ia.

Al - le - lu - ia, al - le - lu - ia, al - le - lú - ia.

D.F.

Chuir an Tiarna uaidh mé ag tabhairt an Dea-Scéil   do na   bochta

ag fógairt a scaoilte   do   bhraighde.

43

Aifreann Eoin Na Croise

CD 1 / Track 22

Peadar ó Riada

Al-le-lu - ia, Al-le-lu - ia o— Al-le-lu - ia.

Le   guth an Tiar - na,   Al - le - lu - ia.

Le guth an Tiar - na,   Al - le - lu - ia.

Ordinary Time (After Christmas)

Aifreann Eoin Na Croise

CD 1 / Track 23

Peadar ó Riada

Al-le-lu - ia, Al-le-lu - ia o— Al-le-lu - ia.

Is tú Pead - ar, Al - le - lu - ia.

Is tú Pead - ar, Al - le - lu - ia.

Ordinary Time
(After Christmas)

Aifreann Eoin Na Croise

CD 1 / Track 24

Peadar ó Riada

Al-le-lu - ia, Al-le-lu- ia o__ Al-le-lu - ia.

Mair-fead bhur dtor - adh, Al - le - lu - ia.

Mair-fead bhur dtor - adh, Al - le - lu - ia.

Aifreann Eoin Na Croise

CD 1 / Track 25

Peadar ó Riada

Al-le-lu - ia, Al-le - lu - ia o— Al-le-lu - ia.

Glan ó chroí,___ Al - le - lu - ia.

Glan ó chroí,__ Al - le - lu - ia.

Aifreann Eoin Na Croise

CD 1 / Track 26

Peadar ó Riada

Al-le-lu - ia, Al-le-lu - ia o— Al-le-lu - ia.

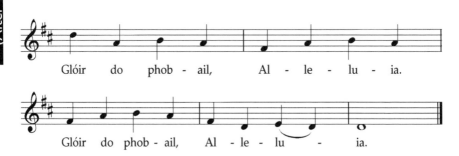

Glóir do phob - ail, Al - le - lu - ia.

Glóir do phob - ail, Al - le - lu - ia.

Aifreann Eoin Na Croise

CD 1 / Track 27

Peadar ó Riada

Al-le-lu - ia, Al-le-lu - ia o— Al-le-lu - ia.

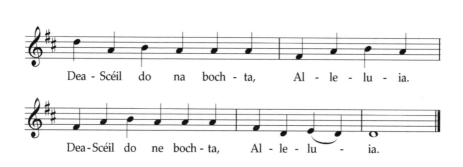

Dea - Scéil do na boch - ta, Al - le - lu - ia.

Dea-Scéil do ne boch - ta, Al - le - lu - ia.

Ordinary Time
(After Christmas)

49

Mass Of The Annunciation

CD 1 / Track 28

Fintan O' Carroll

Al - le - lu - ia, al - le - lu - ia,
al - le - lu - ia, al - le - lu - ia.

D.F.

Blessed are those who hear the word of God

and o - bey it.

Mass Of The Annunciation

CD 1 / Track 29

Fintan O' Carroll

Al - le - lu - ia, al - le - lu - ia, al - le - lu - ia, al - le - lu - ia.

D.F.

I am the light of the world, says the Lord;

whoever follows me will have the light of life.

Ordinary Time
(After Christmas)

Mass Of The Annunciation

CD 1 / Track 30

Fintan O' Carroll

Al - le - lu - ia, al - le - lu - ia, al - le - lu - ia, al - le - lu - ia.

D.F.

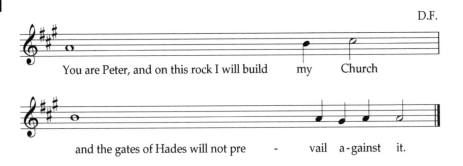

You are Peter, and on this rock I will build my Church and the gates of Hades will not pre - vail a-gainst it.

Ordinary Time (After Christmas)

Mass Of The Annunciation

CD 1 / Track 31

Fintan O' Carroll

Al - le - lu - ia, al - le - lu - ia, al - le - lu - ia, al - le - lu - ia.

D.F.

I chose you.

And I appointed you to go and bear fruit,
fruit that will last, says the Lord.

Mass Of The Annunciation

CD 1 / Track 32

Fintan O' Carroll

Al - le - lu - ia, al - le - lu - ia,
al - le - lu - ia, al - le - lu - ia.

D.F.

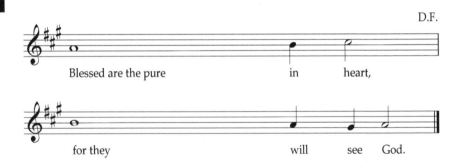

Blessed are the pure in heart,
for they will see God.

Mass Of The Annunciation

CD 1 / Track 33

Fintan O' Carroll

Al - le - lu - ia, al - le - lu - ia,

al - le - lu - ia, al - le - lu - ia.

D.F.

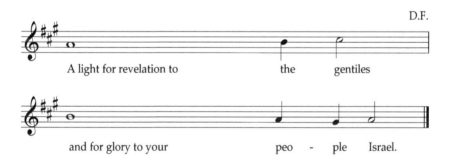

A light for revelation to the gentiles

and for glory to your peo - ple Israel.

55

Mass Of The Annunciation

CD 1 / Track 34

Fintan O' Carroll

Al - le - lu - ia, al - le - lu - ia, al - le - lu - ia, al - le - lu - ia.

D.F.

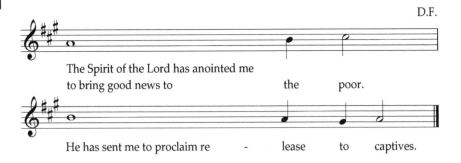

The Spirit of the Lord has anointed me
to bring good news to the poor.

He has sent me to proclaim re - lease to captives.

Mass Of Creation

CD 1 / Track 35

Marty Haugen

Praise to you, Lord Je - sus Christ, king of end - less glo - ry.

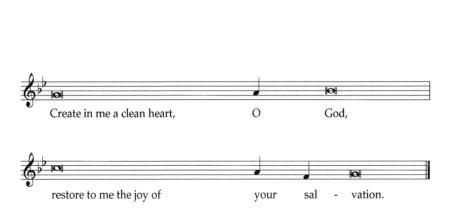

Create in me a clean heart, O God,

restore to me the joy of your sal - vation.

Lent

Mass Of Creation

CD 1 / Track 36

Marty Haugen

Praise to you, Lord Je-sus Christ, king of end-less glo-ry.

D.F.

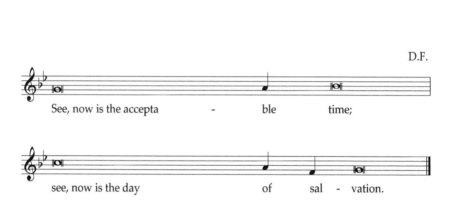

See, now is the accepta - ble time;

see, now is the day of sal - vation.

Aifreann II

CD 1 / Track 37

Bernard Sexton

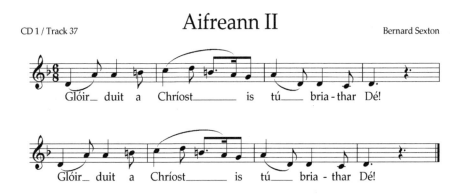

Glóir_ duit a Chríost_____ is tú____ bria - thar Dé!

Glóir_ duit a Chríost_____ is tú____ bria - thar Dé!

D.F.

Chuir an Tiarna uaidh mé ag tabhairt an Dea-Scéil do_____ na bochta

ag fógairt a scaoilte do_____ bhraighde.

Aifreann Eoin Na Croise

CD 1 / Track 38

Peadar ó Riada

Mol-adh duit a Chríost rí na glóire síor-aí ó__ mol-adh duit, a Chríost.

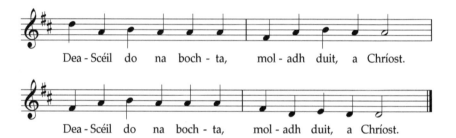

Dea - Scéil do na boch - ta, mol - adh duit, a Chríost.

Dea - Scéil do na boch - ta, mol - adh duit, a Chríost.

Mass Of Creation

CD 1 / Track 39

Marty Haugen

Praise to you, Lord Je-sus Christ, king of end-less glo-ry.

D.F.

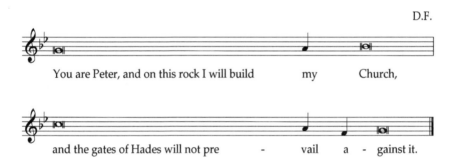

You are Peter, and on this rock I will build my Church,

and the gates of Hades will not pre - vail a - gainst it.

Lent

Mass Of Creation

CD 1 / Track 40

Marty Haugen

Praise to you, Lord Je - sus Christ, king of end - less glo - ry.

D.F.

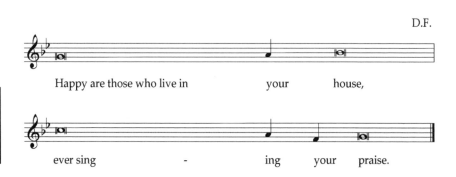

Happy are those who live in your house,

ever sing - ing your praise.

Lent

Mass Of Creation

CD 1 / Track 41

Marty Haugen

Praise to you, Lord Je - sus Christ, king of end - less glo - ry.

D.F.

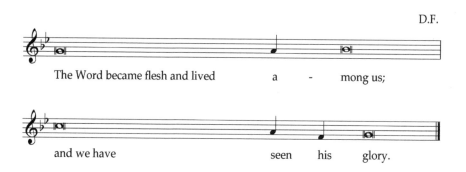

The Word became flesh and lived a - mong us;

and we have seen his glory.

Lent

Mass Of Creation

CD 1 / Track 42

Marty Haugen

Praise to you, Lord Je - sus Christ, king of end - less glo - ry.

D.F.

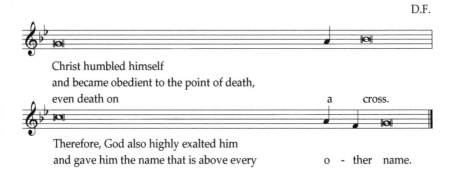

Christ humbled himself
and became obedient to the point of death,
even death on   a   cross.

Therefore, God also highly exalted him
and gave him the name that is above every   o - ther name.

Lent

Mass Of Creation

CD 1 / Track 43

Marty Haugen

Praise to you, Lord Je-sus Christ, king of end-less glo-ry.

D.F.

Hail to you, our King!

You alone have had compassion on our sins.

Lent

Mass Of Creation

CD 1 / Track 44

Marty Haugen

Praise to you, Lord Je - sus Christ, king of end - less glo - ry.

D.F.

The Spirit of the Lord God is u - pon me.

He has anointed me to bring good news to the poor.

CD 1 / Track 45

Saint Benedict's Centenary Mass

Margaret Daly Denton

Praise and ho-nour to you, Lord Je - sus Christ.

I give you a new com - mandment

that you love one an - other

Triduum

CD 1 / Track 46 — **Saint Benedict's Centenary Mass** — Margaret Daly Denton

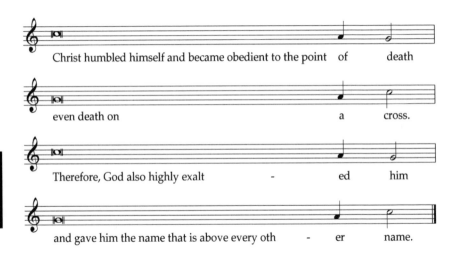

Praise and ho-nour to you, Lord Je-sus Christ.

Christ humbled himself and became obedient to the point of death

even death on a cross.

Therefore, God also highly exalt - ed him

and gave him the name that is above every oth - er name.

Most Reverend Father, I bring you a message of great joy, the message of Alleluia.

CD 1 / Track 47

First Alleluia Of Easter

Plainchant

Al-le - - - lu - ia

Al-le - - - lu - ia

Al-le - - - lu - ia

Triduum

CD 1 / Track 48

Mode VI

Psalm 117: 1-2. 16-17. 22-23

Plainchant

Al - le - lu - ia, al - le - lu - ia - al - le - lu - ia.

M. D.D.

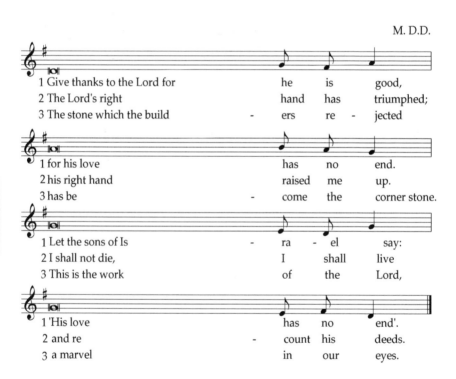

	he	is	good,
1 Give thanks to the Lord for	he	is	good,
2 The Lord's right	hand	has	triumphed;
3 The stone which the build -	ers	re -	jected

1 for his love	has	no	end.
2 his right hand	raised	me	up.
3 has be -	come	the	corner stone.

1 Let the sons of Is -	ra -	el	say:
2 I shall not die,	I	shall	live
3 This is the work	of	the	Lord,

1 'His love	has	no	end'.
2 and re -	count	his	deeds.
3 a marvel	in	our	eyes.

Triduum

CD 1 / Track 49

Mode VI

Plainchant

Psalm 117: 1-2. 16-17. 22-23

Al - le - lu - ia, al - le - lu - ia - al - le - lu - ia.

A. M.

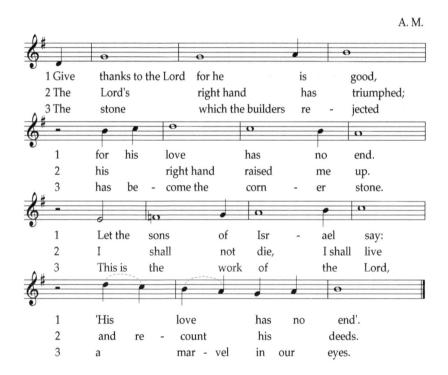

1 Give   thanks to the Lord   for he   is   good,
2 The   Lord's   right hand   has   triumphed;
3 The   stone   which the builders   re -   jected

1   for   his   love   has   no   end.
2   his   right hand   raised   me   up.
3   has   be - come the   corn   -   er   stone.

1   Let the   sons   of   Isr   -   ael   say:
2   I   shall   not   die,   I shall live
3   This is   the   work   of   the   Lord,

1   'His   love   has   no   end'.
2   and   re -   count   his   deeds.
3   a   mar - vel   in   our   eyes.

Triduum

71

Mode VI

CD 1 / Track 50

Plainchant

Al - le - lu - ia, al - le - lu - ia,___ al - le - lu - ia.

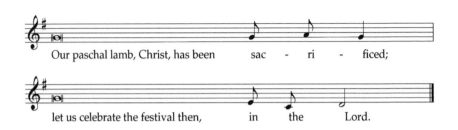

Our paschal lamb, Christ, has been sac - ri - ficed;

let us celebrate the festival then, in the Lord.

Paschal Mass

CD 1 / Track 51

acc. by Richard Proulx

Based on O Filii et Filiae

Al - le - lu - ia,__ Al - le - lu - ia, Al - le - lu - ia.

D. F.

We know that Christ is truly risen from the dead;

have mercy on us, tri - um - phant King.

Paschal Mass

CD 1 / Track 52

Based on O Filii et Filiae

acc. by Richard Proulx

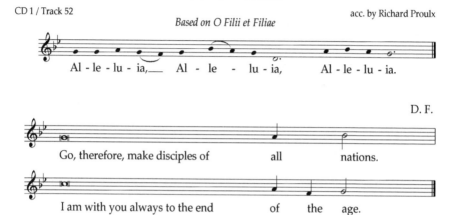

Al - le - lu - ia,___ Al - le - lu - ia, Al - le - lu - ia.

D. F.

Go, therefore, make disciples of all nations.

I am with you always to the end of the age.

Paschal Mass

CD 1 / Track 53

acc. by Richard Proulx

Based on O Filii et Filiae

Al - le - lu - ia,__ Al - le - lu - ia, Al - le - lu - ia.

D. F.

Come, Holy Spirit, fill the hearts of   your   faithful

and kindle in them the fire   of   your   love.

Mass Of God's Promise

CD 1 / Track 54

Daniel L. Schutte

Al - le - lu - ia, al - le - lu - ia, al - le - lu - ia.

D.F.

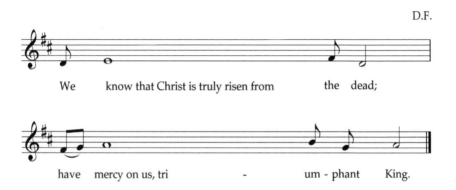

We   know that Christ is truly risen from   the dead;

have   mercy on us, tri   -   um - phant   King.

Easter

Mass Of God's Promise

CD 1 / Track 55

Daniel L. Schutte

Al - le - lu - ia, al - le - lu - ia, al - le - lu - ia.

D.F.

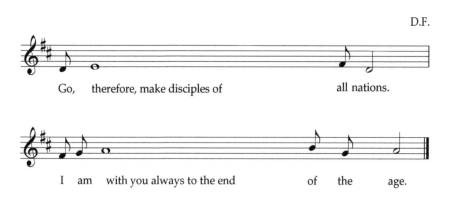

Go, therefore, make disciples of   all nations.

I am with you always to the end   of the age.

Easter

Mass Of God's Promise

CD 1 / Track 56

Daniel L. Schutte

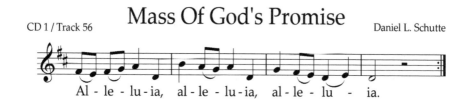

Al - le - lu - ia, al - le - lu - ia, al - le - lu - ia.

D.F.

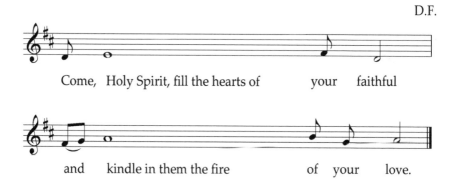

Come, Holy Spirit, fill the hearts of   your   faithful

and   kindle in them the fire   of   your   love.

Easter

Mode VI

CD 1 / Track 57

Plainchant

Al - le - lu - ia,   al - le - lu - ia,____   al - le - lu - ia.

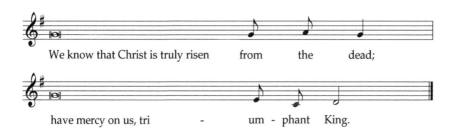

We know that Christ is truly risen   from   the   dead;

have mercy on us, tri   -   um - phant King.

Easter

79

Mode VI

CD 1 / Track 58

Plainchant

Al - le - lu - ia,   al - le - lu - ia,___   al - le - lu - ia.

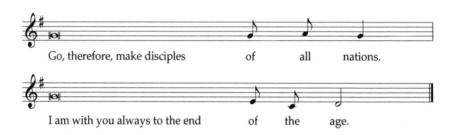

Go, therefore, make disciples   of   all   nations.

I am with you always to the end   of   the   age.

Mode VI

CD 1 / Track 59

Plainchant

Al - le - lu - ia, al - le - lu - ia, al - le - lu - ia.

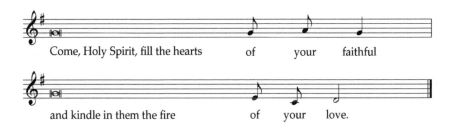

Come, Holy Spirit, fill the hearts of your faithful

and kindle in them the fire of your love.

Easter

Mass Of Saint Finbarr

CD 1 / Track 60

Patrick Killeen

Al - le - lu - ia, Al - le - lu - ia, Al - le - lu - ia___ Al - le - lu - ia.

Tone 2

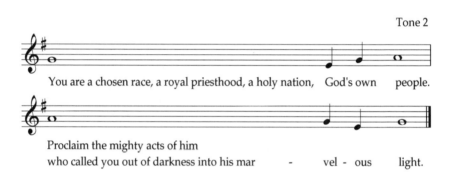

You are a chosen race, a royal priesthood, a holy nation, God's own people.

Proclaim the mighty acts of him
who called you out of darkness into his mar - vel - ous light.

Mass Of Saint Finbarr

CD 1 / Track 61

Patrick Killeen

Al - le - lu - ia, Al - le - lu - ia, Al - le - lu - ia___ Al - le - lu - ia.

Tone 2

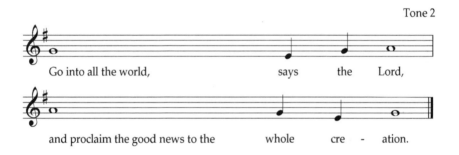

Go into all the world, says the Lord,

and proclaim the good news to the whole cre - ation.

Mass Of Saint Finbarr

CD 1 / Track 62

Patrick Killeen

Al - le - lu - ia, Al - le - lu - ia, Al - le - lu - ia___ Al - le - lu - ia.

Tone 2

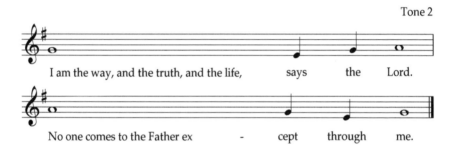

I am the way, and the truth, and the life, says the Lord.

No one comes to the Father ex - cept through me.

Mass Of Saint Finbarr

CD 1 / Track 63

Patrick Killeen

Al - le - lu - ia, Al - le - lu - ia, Al - le - lu - ia___ Al - le - lu - ia.

Tone 2

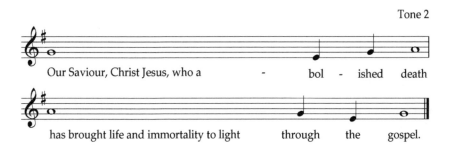

Our Saviour, Christ Jesus, who a - bol - ished death

has brought life and immortality to light through the gospel.

Mass Of Saint Finbarr

CD 1 / Track 64

Patrick Killeen

Al - le - lu - ia,   Al - le - lu - ia,   Al - le - lu - ia___ Al - le - lu - ia.

Tone 2

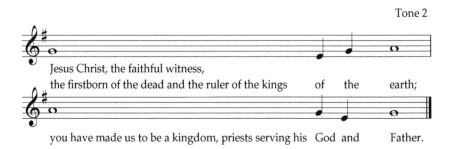

Jesus Christ, the faithful witness,
the firstborn of the dead and the ruler of the kings   of   the   earth;

you have made us to be a kingdom, priests serving his God and   Father.

Paschal Mass

Based on O Filii et Filiae

CD 1 / Track 65

acc. by Richard Proulx

Al - le - lu - ia,___ Al - le - lu - ia, Al - le - lu - ia.

D. F.

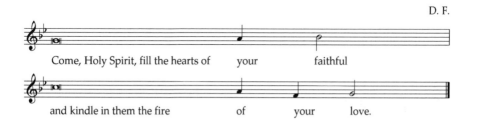

Come, Holy Spirit, fill the hearts of your faithful

and kindle in them the fire of your love.

Christian Initiation

Mass Of God's Promise

CD 1 / Track 66

Daniel L. Schutte

Al - le - lu - ia, al - le - lu - ia, al - le - lu - ia.

D.F.

Come, Holy Spirit, fill the hearts of   your faithful

and   kindle in them the fire   of   your   love.

Mode VI

CD 1 / Track 67

Plainchant

Al - le - lu - ia,   al - le - lu - ia,___ al - le - lu - ia.

Come, Holy Spirit, fill the hearts   of   your   faithful

and kindle in them the fire   of   your   love.

Mass Of Saint Finbarr

CD 1 / Track 68

Patrick Killeen

Al - le - lu - ia,   Al - le - lu - ia,   Al - le - lu - ia___ Al - le - lu - ia.

Tone 2

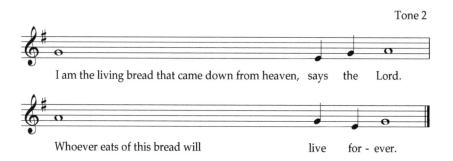

I am the living bread that came down from heaven, says   the   Lord.

Whoever eats of this bread will   live   for - ever.

Mass Of Saint Finbarr

CD 1 / Track 69

Patrick Killeen

Al - le - lu - ia, Al - le - lu - ia, Al - le - lu - ia___ Al - le - lu - ia.

Tone 2

If you continue in my word, you are truly my dis - ciples;

and you will know the truth,
and the truth will make you free.

Mass Of Saint Finbarr

CD 1 / Track 70

Patrick Killeen

Al - le - lu - ia, Al - le - lu - ia, Al - le - lu - ia___ Al - le - lu - ia.

Tone 2

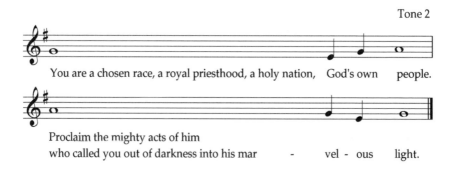

You are a chosen race, a royal priesthood, a holy nation, God's own people.

Proclaim the mighty acts of him
who called you out of darkness into his mar - vel - ous light.

CD 1 / Track 71

Mass Of The Annunciation

Fintan O' Carroll

Al - le - lu - ia, al - le - lu - ia,

al - le - lu - ia, al - le - lu - ia.

D.F.

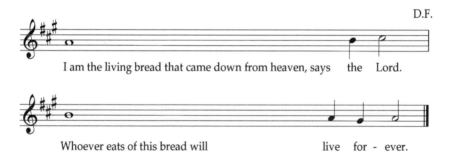

I am the living bread that came down from heaven, says the Lord.

Whoever eats of this bread will live for - ever.

Christian
Initiation

Mass Of Saint John Of The Cross

CD 1 / Track 72 — R. McDonagh

Al - le - lu - ia, al - le - lu - ia, al - le - lu - ia.

D.F.

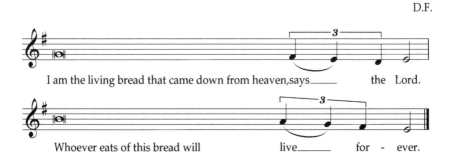

I am the living bread that came down from heaven, says___ the Lord.

Whoever eats of this bread will live___ for - ever.

Mass Of Saint Finbarr

CD 2 / Track 1

Patrick Killeen

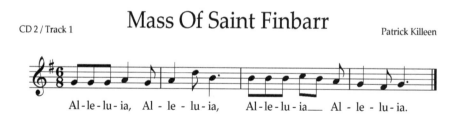

Al - le - lu - ia, Al - le - lu - ia, Al - le - lu - ia__ Al - le - lu - ia.

Tone 2

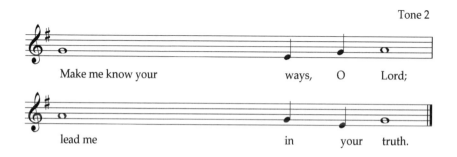

Make me know your ways, O Lord;

lead me in your truth.

Ordinary Time
(After Easter)

Mass Of Saint Finbarr

CD 2 / Track 2

Patrick Killeen

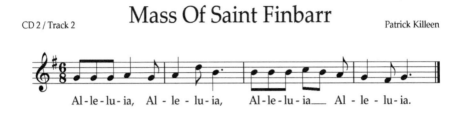

Al - le - lu - ia, Al - le - lu - ia, Al - le - lu - ia___ Al - le - lu - ia.

Tone 2

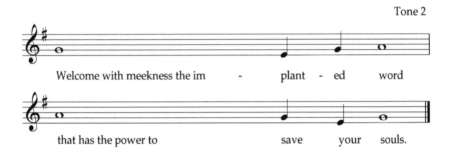

Welcome with meekness the im - plant - ed word

that has the power to save your souls.

Mass Of Saint Finbarr

CD 2 / Track 3

Patrick Killeen

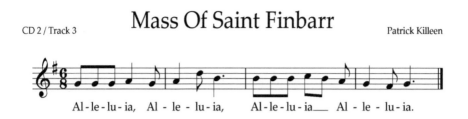

Al - le - lu - ia, Al - le - lu - ia, Al - le - lu - ia___ Al - le - lu - ia.

Tone 1

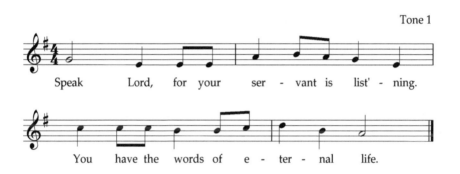

Speak Lord, for your ser - vant is list' - ning.

You have the words of e - ter - nal life.

Mass Of The Annunciation

CD 2 / Track 4

Fintan O' Carroll

Al - le - lu - ia, al - le - lu - ia,
al - le - lu - ia, al - le - lu - ia.

D.F.

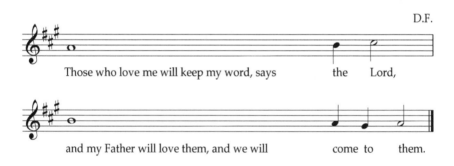

Those who love me will keep my word, says the Lord,

and my Father will love them, and we will come to them.

Mass Of The Annunciation

CD 2 / Track 5

Fintan O' Carroll

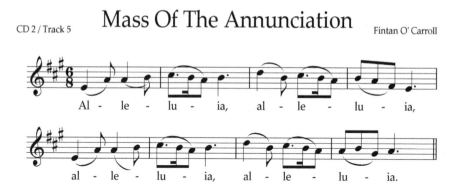

Al - le - lu - ia, al - le - lu - ia,

al - le - lu - ia, al - le - lu - ia.

D.F.

I am the light of the world, says the Lord,

whoever follows me will have the light of life.

Ordinary Time
(After Easter)

Mass Of The Annunciation

CD 2 / Track 6

Fintan O' Carroll

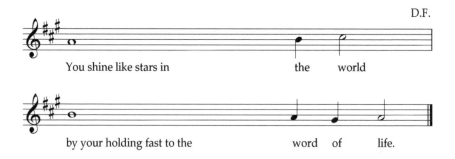

Al - le - lu - ia, al - le - lu - ia,

al - le - lu - ia, al - le - lu - ia.

D.F.

You shine like stars in the world

by your holding fast to the word of life.

CD 2 / Track 7 **Mass Of Saint John Of The Cross** R. McDonagh

Al - le-lu - ia,   al - le - lu - ia,   al - le - lu - ia.

D.F.

One does not live by   bread___   a - lone,

but by every word that comes from the   mouth___   of   God.

CD 2 / Track 8 **Mass Of Saint John Of The Cross** R. McDonagh

Al - le - lu - ia, al - le - lu - ia, al - le - lu - ia.

D.F.

Make me understand the way of your precepts

and I will meditate on your won - drous works.

CD 2 / Track 9 # Mass Of Saint John Of The Cross R. McDonagh

Al - le-lu - ia, al - le - lu - ia, al - le - lu - ia.

D.F.

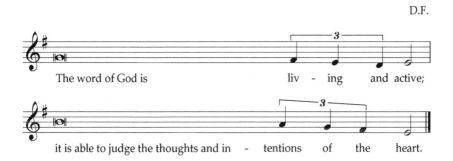

The word of God is liv - ing and active;

it is able to judge the thoughts and in - tentions of the heart.

CD 2 / Track 10

Sacred Story

Liam Lawton

Al-le-lu - ia, Al-le-lu - ia, Al - le-lu - ia

Al - le-lu - ia, Al - le-lu - ia, Al - le-lu - ia!

The_ Lord has sent me with good news; the won - der of sal - va - tion. Pro -

claim - ing jus - tice, love and_truth. Go forth_ to ev' - ry na - tion.

Mass Of The Annunciation

CD 2 / Track 11

Fintan O' Carroll

Al - le - lu - ia, al - le - lu - ia,

al - le - lu - ia, al - le - lu - ia.

D.F.

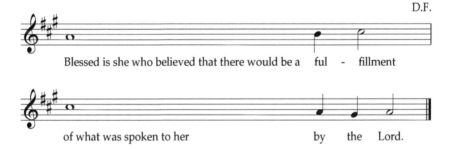

Blessed is she who believed that there would be a ful - fillment

of what was spoken to her by the Lord.

Ordinary Time
(After Easter)

Mass Of Saint Finbarr

CD 2 / Track 12

Patrick Killeen

Al-le-lu-ia, Al - le - lu-ia, Al-le-lu-ia___ Al - le - lu-ia.

Tone 2

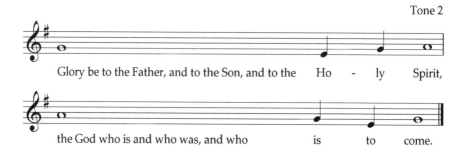

Glory be to the Father, and to the Son, and to the Ho - ly Spirit,

the God who is and who was, and who is to come.

Mass Of The Annunciation

CD 2 / Track 13

Fintan O' Carroll

Al - le - lu - ia, al - le - lu - ia,

al - le - lu - ia, al - le - lu - ia.

D.F.

Glory be to the Father, and to the Son, and to the Ho - ly Spirit,

the God who is and who was, and who is to come.

Mass Of Saint John Of The Cross

R. McDonagh

Al - le-lu - ia, al - le - lu - ia, al - le - lu - ia.

D.F.

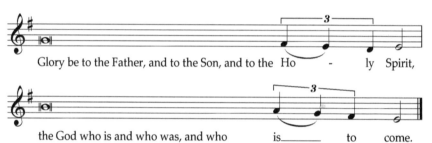

Glory be to the Father, and to the Son, and to the Ho - ly Spirit,

the God who is and who was, and who is___ to come.

Mass Of Saint Finbarr

CD 2 / Track 15

Patrick Killeen

Al - le - lu - ia, Al - le - lu - ia, Al - le - lu - ia ___ Al - le - lu - ia.

Tone 2

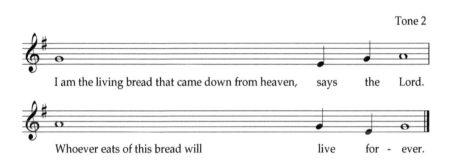

I am the living bread that came down from heaven, says the Lord.

Whoever eats of this bread will live for - ever.

Ordinary Time
(After Easter)

Mass Of The Annunciation

CD 2 / Track 16

Fintan O' Carroll

Al - le - lu - ia, al - le - lu - ia,
al - le - lu - ia, al - le - lu - ia.

D.F.

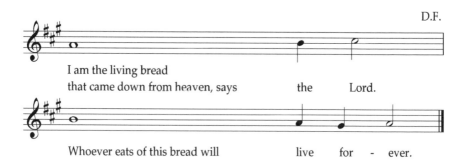

I am the living bread
that came down from heaven, says the Lord.

Whoever eats of this bread will live for - ever.

CD 2 / Track 17 # Mass Of Saint John Of The Cross R. McDonagh

Al - le-lu - ia, al - le - lu - ia, al - le - lu - ia.

D.F.

I am the living bread
that came down from heaven, says___ the Lord.

Whoever eats of this bread will live___ for - ever.

CD 2 / Track 18 # Mass Of Saint John Of The Cross R. McDonagh

Al - le-lu - ia, al - le - lu - ia, al - le - lu - ia.

D.F.

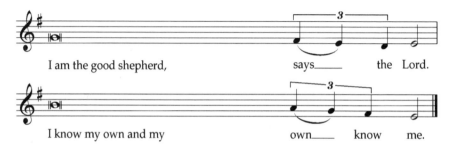

I am the good shepherd, says___ the Lord.

I know my own and my own___ know me.

Mass Of Saint Finbarr

CD 2 / Track 19

Patrick Killeen

Al - le - lu - ia, Al - le - lu - ia, Al - le - lu - ia___ Al - le - lu - ia.

Tone 2

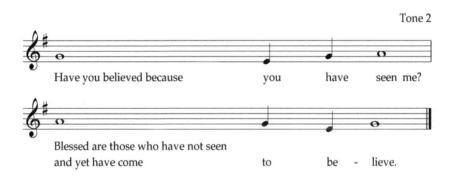

Have you believed because you have seen me?

Blessed are those who have not seen
and yet have come to be - lieve.

* For Saints Mark, Philip & James and Matthias, celebrated in the Season of Easter, use the acclamation text above, but sing it according to the *Alleluia* refrain and *verse* tone of either *Paschal Mass*, *Mass Of God's Promise* or *Mode VI*.

• When the Feast of Saint Matthias is celebrated in Ordinary Time after Easter, use the setting above from the *Mass Of Saint Finbarr*

Ordinary Time
(After Easter)

Ordinary Time after the Season of Easter
Saints Mark*, Philip and James*, Matthias* •, Barnabas, Thomas, James, Bartholomew, Mathew, Luke, Simon and Jude, Andrew.

Mass Of The Annunciation

CD 2 / Track 20

Fintan O' Carroll

Al - le - lu - ia, al - le - lu - ia,
al - le - lu - ia, al - le - lu - ia.

D.F.

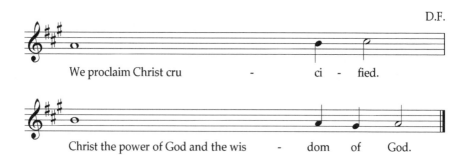

We proclaim Christ cru - ci - fied.

Christ the power of God and the wis - dom of God.

Ordinary Time after the Season of Easter
Saints Mark*, Philip and James*, Matthias* •, Barnabas, Thomas, James, Bartholomew, Mathew, Luke, Simon and Jude, Andrew.

CD 2 / Track 21 # Mass Of Saint John Of The Cross R. McDonagh

Al - le-lu - ia, al - le - lu - ia, al - le - lu - ia.

D.F.

You did not choose me, but I chose you,

and I appointed you to go and bear fruit, fruit that will last.

Mass Of Saint Finbarr

CD 2 / Track 22

Patrick Killeen

Al - le - lu - ia,   Al - le - lu - ia,   Al - le - lu - ia___ Al - le - lu - ia.

Tone 2

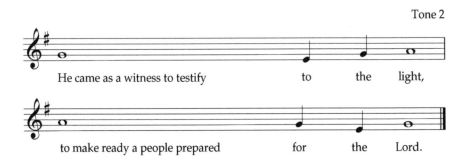

He came as a witness to testify   to   the   light,

to make ready a people prepared   for   the   Lord.

Mass Of The Annunciation

CD 2 / Track 23

Fintan O' Carroll

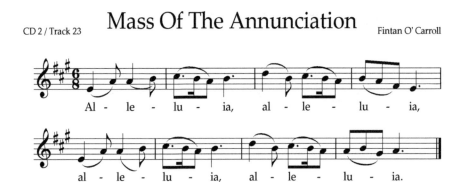

Al - le - lu - ia, al - le - lu - ia,

al - le - lu - ia, al - le - lu - ia.

D.F.

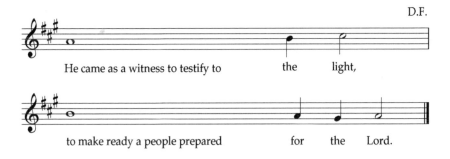

He came as a witness to testify to the light,

to make ready a people prepared for the Lord.

Ordinary Time
(After Easter)

CD 2 / Track 24 # Mass Of Saint John Of The Cross R. McDonagh

Al - le - lu - ia, al - le - lu - ia, al - le - lu - ia.

D.F.

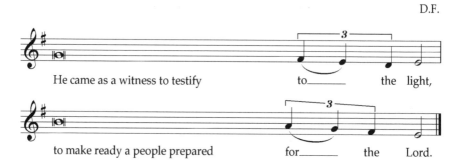

He came as a witness to testify to_____ the light,

to make ready a people prepared for_____ the Lord.

Mass Of Saint Finbarr

CD 2 / Track 25

Patrick Killeen

Al -le -lu- ia, Al - le - lu- ia,   Al -le -lu- ia___ Al - le - lu- ia.

Tone 2

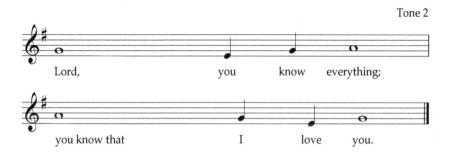

Lord,   you   know   everything;

you know that   I   love   you.

Mass Of The Annunciation

CD 2 / Track 26

Fintan O' Carroll

Al - le - lu - ia, al - le - lu - ia,

al - le - lu - ia, al - le - lu - ia.

D.F.

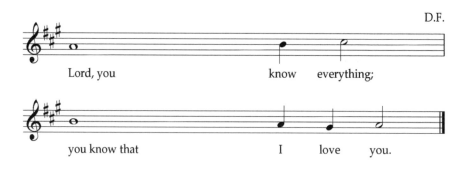

Lord, you know everything;

you know that I love you.

CD 2 / Track 27

Mass Of Saint John Of The Cross

R. McDonagh

Al - le-lu - ia, al - le - lu - ia, al - le - lu - ia.

D.F.

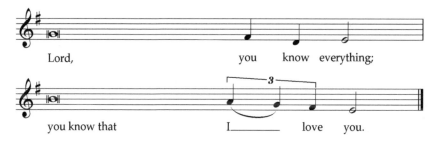

Lord, you know everything;

you know that I_____ love you.

Ordinary Time after the Season of Easter
Saints Columba (Colum Cille), Benedict, Bridget of Sweden, Teresa Benedict of the Cross (Edith Stein), Lawrence and Catherine of Siena*

Mass Of Saint Finbarr

CD 2 / Track 28

Patrick Killeen

Al - le - lu - ia, Al - le - lu - ia,   Al - le - lu - ia___ Al - le - lu - ia.

Tone 2

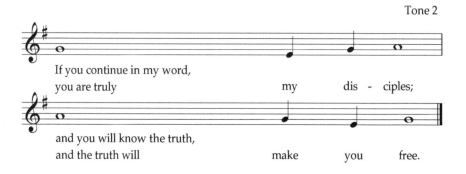

If you continue in my word,
you are truly   my   dis - ciples;

and you will know the truth,
and the truth will   make   you   free.

* For Saint Catherine of Siena, celebrated in the Season of Easter, use the acclamation text above, but sing it according to the *Alleluia* refrain and **verse** tone of either *Paschal Mass, Mass Of God's Promise or Mode VI*

Ordinary Time after the Season of Easter
Saints Columba (Colum Cille), Benedict, Bridget of Sweden,
Teresa Benedict of the Cross (Edith Stein), Lawrence and
Catherine of Siena*

Mass Of The Annunciation

CD 2 / Track 29

Fintan O' Carroll

Al - le - lu - ia, al - le - lu - ia,
al - le - lu - ia, al - le - lu - ia.

D.F.

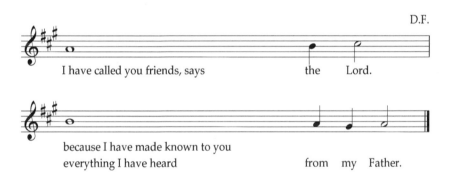

I have called you friends, says the Lord.

because I have made known to you
everything I have heard from my Father.

* For Saint Catherine of Siena, celebrated in the Season of Easter, use the acclamation text above, but sing it according to the *Alleluia* refrain and **verse** tone of either *Paschal Mass, Mass Of God's Promise or Mode VI*

Ordinary Time
(After Easter)

Ordinary Time after the Season of Easter
Saints Columba (Colum Cille), Benedict, Bridget of Sweden, Teresa Benedict of the Cross (Edith Stein), Lawrence and Catherine of Siena*

CD 2 / Track 30 ## Mass Of Saint John Of The Cross R. McDonagh

Al - le-lu - ia, al - le - lu - ia, al - le - lu - ia.

D.F.

If you are reviled for the name of Christ,   you____ are blessed,

because the spirit of glory,
which is the Spirit of God, is   rest - ing on you.

* For Saint Catherine of Siena, celebrated in the Season of Easter, use the acclamation text above, but sing it according to the *Alleluia* refrain and **verse** tone of either *Paschal Mass, Mass Of God's Promise or Mode VI*

CD 2 / Track 31 # Mass Of Saint John Of The Cross R. McDonagh

Al - le-lu - ia, al - le - lu - ia, al - le - lu - ia.

D.F.

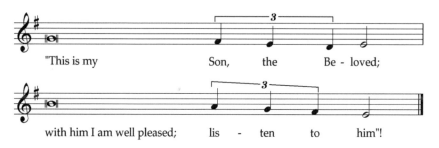

"This is my Son, the Be - loved;

with him I am well pleased; lis - ten to him"!

Mass Of Saint Finbarr

CD 2 / Track 32

Patrick Killeen

Al-le-lu-ia, Al - le - lu-ia, Al-le-lu-ia— Al - le - lu-ia.

Tone 2

Blessed are those who hear the word of God

and o - bey it.

Mass Of The Annunciation

CD 2 / Track 33

Fintan O' Carroll

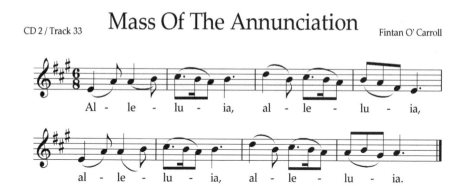

Al - le - lu - ia, al - le - lu - ia, al - le - lu - ia, al - le - lu - ia.

D.F.

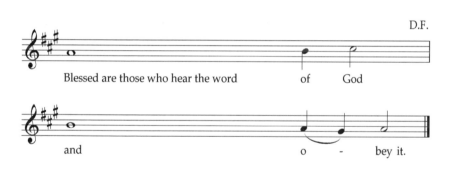

Blessed are those who hear the word of God and o - bey it.

Ordinary Time (After Easter)

Mass Of Saint John Of The Cross

CD 2 / Track 34

R. McDonagh

Al - le-lu - ia, al - le - lu - ia, al - le-lu - ia.

D.F.

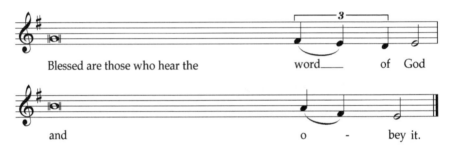

Blessed are those who hear the word____ of God and o - bey it.

Ordinary Time after the Season of Easter
The Solemnity of the Assumption of the Blessed Virgin Mary
(During the Day)

Mass Of Saint Finbarr

CD 2 / Track 35

Patrick Killeen

Al - le - lu - ia, Al - le - lu - ia, Al - le - lu - ia__ Al - le - lu - ia.

Tone 2

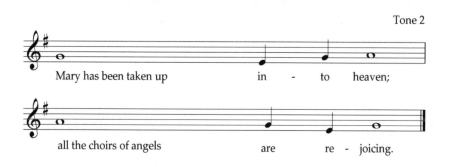

Mary has been taken up   in - to   heaven;

all the choirs of angels   are   re - joicing.

Ordinary Time after the Season of Easter
The Solemnity of the Assumption of the Blessed Virgin Mary
(During the Day)

Mass Of The Annunciation

CD 2 / Track 36

Fintan O' Carroll

Al - le - lu - ia, al - le - lu - ia, al - le - lu - ia, al - le - lu - ia.

D.F.

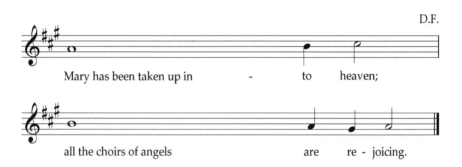

Mary has been taken up in - to heaven; all the choirs of angels are re - joicing.

Ordinary Time after the Season of Easter
The Solemnity of the Assumption of the Blessed Virgin Mary
(During the Day)

CD 2 / Track 37 # Mass Of Saint John Of The Cross R. McDonagh

Al - le-lu - ia, al - le - lu - ia, al - le - lu - ia.

D.F.

Mary has been taken up in - to heaven;

all the choirs of angels are re - joi - cing.

Mass Of Saint Finbarr

CD 2 / Track 38

Patrick Killeen

Al - le - lu - ia, Al - le - lu - ia, Al - le - lu - ia___ Al - le - lu - ia.

Tone 2

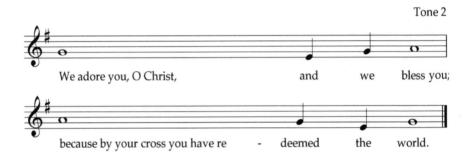

We adore you, O Christ,   and   we   bless you;

because by your cross you have re   -   deemed   the   world.

Mass Of The Annunciation

CD 2 / Track 39

Fintan O' Carroll

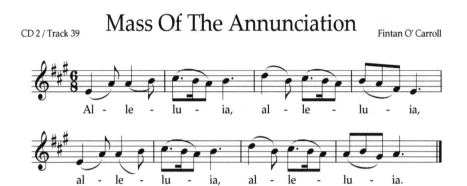

Al - le - lu - ia, al - le - lu - ia,
al - le - lu - ia, al - le - lu - ia.

D.F.

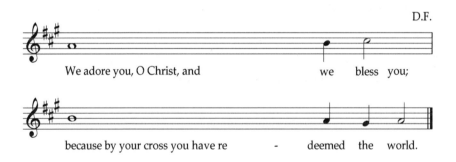

We adore you, O Christ, and we bless you;

because by your cross you have re - deemed the world.

Ordinary Time (After Easter)

CD 2 / Track 40 # Mass Of Saint John Of The Cross R. McDonagh

Al - le-lu - ia, al - le-lu - ia, al - le-lu - ia.

D.F.

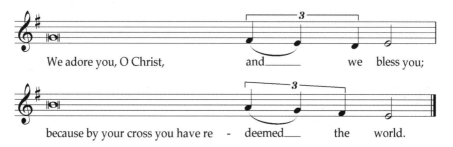

We adore you, O Christ, and we bless you;

because by your cross you have re - deemed the world.

Mass Of Saint Finbarr

CD 2 / Track 41

Patrick Killeen

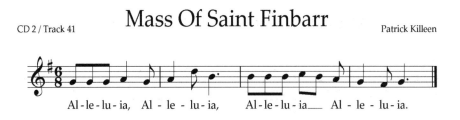

Al - le - lu - ia, Al - le - lu - ia, Al - le - lu - ia___ Al - le - lu - ia.

Tone 2

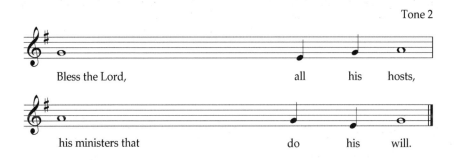

Bless the Lord, all his hosts,

his ministers that do his will.

Mass Of The Annunciation

CD 2 / Track 42

Fintan O' Carroll

Al - le - lu - ia, al - le - lu - ia,

al - le - lu - ia, al - le - lu - ia.

D.F.

Bless the Lord, all his hosts,

his ministers that do his will.

CD 2 / Track 43 # Mass Of Saint John Of The Cross R. McDonagh

Al - le - lu - ia, al - le - lu - ia, al - le - lu - ia.

D.F.

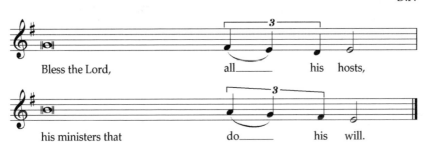

Bless the Lord, all___ his hosts,

his ministers that do___ his will.

Ordinary Time
(After Easter)

Mass Of The Annunciation

CD 2 / Track 44

Fintan O' Carroll

Al - le - lu - ia, al - le - lu - ia,

al - le - lu - ia, al - le - lu - ia.

D.F.

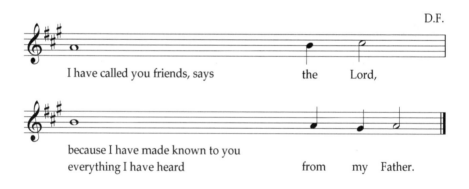

I have called you friends, says   the   Lord,

because I have made known to you
everything I have heard   from   my   Father.

Mass Of Saint Finbarr

CD 2 / Track 45

Patrick Killeen

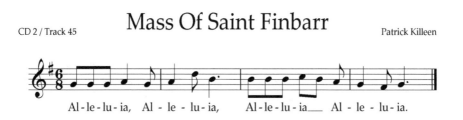

Al - le - lu - ia, Al - le - lu - ia, Al - le - lu - ia___ Al - le - lu - ia.

Tone 2

Come to me, all you that are weary
and are carrying   hea - vy   burdens,

and I will   give   you   rest.

Mass Of The Annunciation

CD 2 / Track 46

Fintan O' Carroll

Al - le - lu - ia, al - le - lu - ia,
al - le - lu - ia, al - le - lu - ia.

D.F.

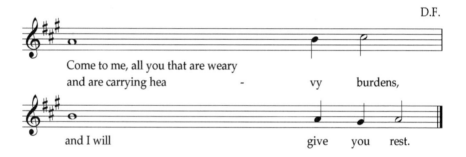

Come to me, all you that are weary
and are carrying hea - vy burdens,

and I will give you rest.

CD 2 / Track 47 # Mass Of Saint John Of The Cross R. McDonagh

Al - le-lu - ia, al - le - lu - ia, al - le - lu - ia.

D.F.

Come to me, all you that are weary
and are carrying   hea - vy   burdens,

and I will   give___ you   rest.

Mass Of Saint Finbarr

CD 2 / Track 48

Patrick Killeen

Al - le - lu - ia,   Al - le - lu - ia,   Al - le - lu - ia___ Al - le - lu - ia.

Tone 2

This is the will of him who sent me,   says   the   Lord.

That I should lose nothing
of all that he has given me,
but raise it up on   the   last   day.

CD 2 / Track 49

Mass Of The Annunciation

Fintan O' Carroll

Al - le - lu - ia, al - le - lu - ia,
al - le - lu - ia, al - le - lu - ia.

D.F.

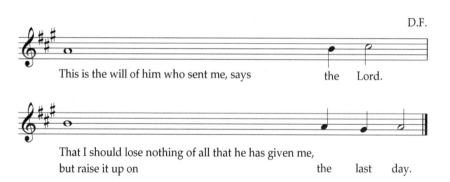

This is the will of him who sent me, says the Lord.

That I should lose nothing of all that he has given me,
but raise it up on the last day.

CD 2 / Track 50 # Mass Of Saint John Of The Cross   R. McDonagh

Al - le-lu - ia, al - le - lu - ia, al - le - lu - ia.

D.F.

This is the will of him who sent me,   says the Lord.

That I should lose nothing
of all that he has given me, but raise it up   on   the   last   day.

Mass Of Saint Finbarr

CD 2 / Track 51

Patrick Killeen

Al - le - lu - ia, Al - le - lu - ia, Al - le - lu - ia___ Al - le - lu - ia.

Tone 2

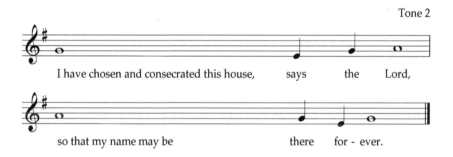

I have chosen and consecrated this house, says the Lord,

so that my name may be there for - ever.

Ordinary Time
(After Easter)

Mass Of The Annunciation

CD 2 / Track 52

Fintan O' Carroll

Al - le - lu - ia, al - le - lu - ia,

al - le - lu - ia, al - le - lu - ia.

D.F.

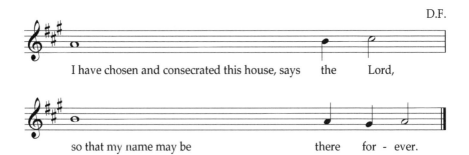

I have chosen and consecrated this house, says the Lord,

so that my name may be there for - ever.

CD 2 / Track 53 **Mass Of Saint John Of The Cross** R. McDonagh

Al - le-lu - ia, al - le - lu - ia, al - le - lu - ia.

D.F.

I have chosen and consecrated this house, says____ the Lord,

so that my name may be there____ for - ever.

Mass Of Saint Finbarr

CD 2 / Track 54

Patrick Killeen

Al - le - lu - ia, Al - le - lu - ia, Al - le - lu - ia___ Al - le - lu - ia.

Tone 2

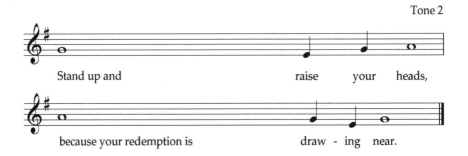

Stand up and raise your heads,

because your redemption is draw - ing near.

CD 2 / Track 55

Mass Of The Annunciation

Fintan O' Carroll

Al - le - lu - ia, al - le - lu - ia, al - le - lu - ia, al - le - lu - ia.

D.F.

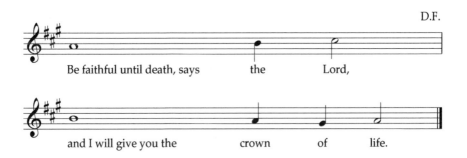

Be faithful until death, says the Lord, and I will give you the crown of life.

Ordinary Time after the Season of Easter
The Thirty-Second and the Thirty-Third Sundays / Weeks in
Ordinary Time

CD 2 / Track 56 **Mass Of Saint John Of The Cross** R. McDonagh

Al - le-lu - ia, al - le-lu - ia, al - le-lu - ia.

D.F.

Be alert   at___ all times,

praying
that you may have the strength to stand before the Son___ of Man.

Mass Of Saint Finbarr

CD 2 / Track 57

Patrick Killeen

Al - le - lu - ia, Al - le - lu - ia, Al - le - lu - ia___ Al - le - lu - ia.

Tone 2

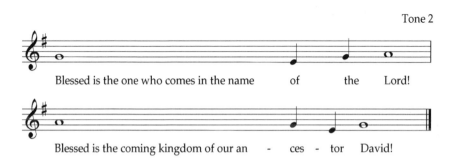

Blessed is the one who comes in the name of the Lord!

Blessed is the coming kingdom of our an - ces - tor David!

Mass Of The Annunciation

CD 2 / Track 58

Fintan O' Carroll

Al - le - lu - ia, al - le - lu - ia, al - le - lu - ia, al - le - lu - ia.

D.F.

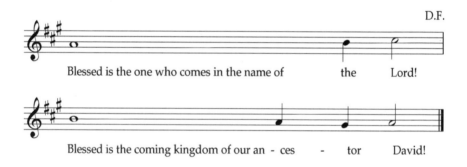

Blessed is the one who comes in the name of the Lord!

Blessed is the coming kingdom of our an - ces - tor David!

CD 2 / Track 59 # Mass Of Saint John Of The Cross R. McDonagh

Al - le - lu - ia, al - le - lu - ia, al - le - lu - ia.

D.F.

Blessed is the one who comes in the name of the Lord!

Blessed is the coming kingdom of our an - ces - tor David!

Ordinary Time
(After Easter)

Mass Of God's Promise

CD 2 / Track 60

Daniel L. Schutte

Al - le - lu - ia, al - le - lu - ia, al - le - lu - ia.

D.F.

God is love;

since God loved us so much, we also, ought to love one an - other.

Mass Of Saint Finbarr

CD 2 / Track 61

Patrick Killeen

Al - le - lu - ia, Al - le - lu - ia, Al - le - lu - ia___ Al - le - lu - ia.

Tone 2

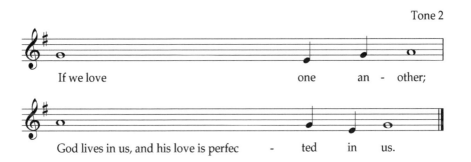

If we love one an - other;

God lives in us, and his love is perfec - ted in us.

Mass For The People

CD 2 / Track 62

Mary Pedder Daly

Al - le - lu - ia, al - le - lu - ia, al - le - lu - u - ia.

al - le - lu - ia, al - le - lu - ia, al - le - lu____ ia.

God is love,

and those who abide in love abide in God,
and God   a - bides   in   them.

Aifreann II

CD 2 / Track 63

Bernard Sexton

Al - le -lu - ia, al - le - lu - ia, Al - le - lu - ia.

Al - le - lu - ia, al - le - lu - ia, al - le - lu - ia.

D.F.

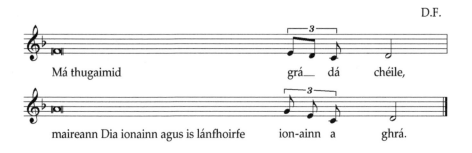

Má thugaimid grá— dá chéile,

maireann Dia ionainn agus is lánfhoirfe ion-ainn a ghrá.

Marriage

157

Aifreann Eoin Na Croise

CD 2 / Track 64

Peadar ó Riada

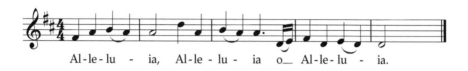

Al-le-lu - ia, Al-le-lu - ia o_ Al-le-lu - ia.

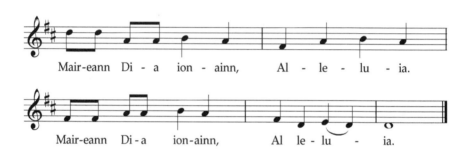

Mair-eann Di - a ion - ainn, Al - le - lu - ia.

Mair-eann Di - a ion-ainn, Al le-lu - ia.

Mass Of Creation

CD 2 / Track 65

Marty Haugen

Praise to you, Lord Je-sus Christ, King of end-less glo - ry.

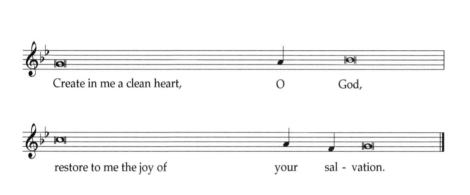

Create in me a clean heart,   O   God,

restore to me the joy of   your   sal - vation.

Penance

Mass Of Saint Finbarr

CD 2 / Track 66

Patrick Killeen

Al - le - lu - ia, Al - le - lu - ia, Al - le - lu - ia___ Al - le - lu - ia.

Tone 2

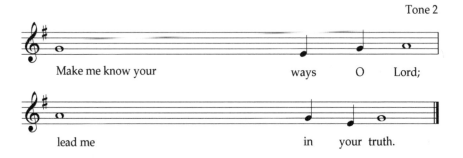

Make me know your ways O Lord;

lead me in your truth.

CD 2 / Track 67

Alleluia - Magnificat

Lécot / Décha

Al - le - lu - ia, al - le - lu - ia, al - le - lu - ia!

M. Mc S.

Look, the Lord will come to save his people.

Blessed those who are ready to meet him.

Funerals

Mass Of Peace

CD 2 / Track 68

Seóirse Bodley

Al - le - lu - ia. Al - le - lu - ia. Al - le - lu - ia.

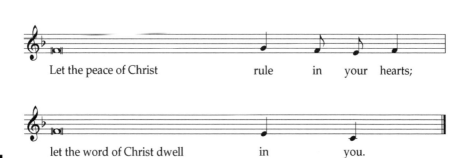

Let the peace of Christ   rule   in   your hearts;

let the word of Christ dwell   in   you.

Mass Of Light

CD 2 / Track 69

David Haas

Al - le - lu - ia.   al - le - lu - ia,   al - le - lu - ia.

Al - le - lu - ia,   al - le - lu - ia,   al - le - lu ia.

D. F.

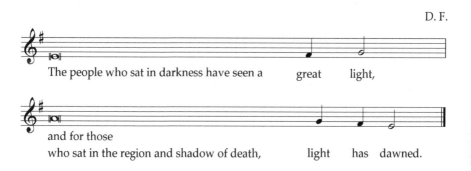

The people who sat in darkness have seen a   great   light,

and for those
who sat in the region and shadow of death,   light   has   dawned.

Funerals

Mass Of Creation

CD 2 / Track 70

Marty Haugen

Praise to you, Lord Je-sus Christ, King of end-less glo-ry.

D.F.

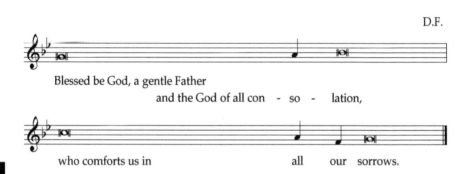

Blessed be God, a gentle Father
and the God of all con - so - lation,

who comforts us in all our sorrows.

Funerals

Mass Of Creation

CD 2 / Track 71

Marty Haugen

Praise to you, Lord Je-sus Christ, king of end-less glo-ry.

D.F.

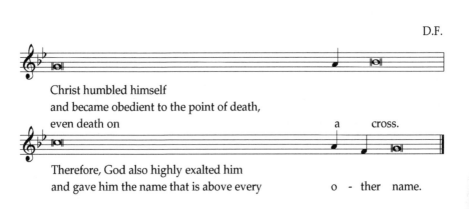

Christ humbled himself
and became obedient to the point of death,
even death on   a   cross.

Therefore, God also highly exalted him
and gave him the name that is above every   o - ther name.

Aifreann II

CD 2 / Track 72

Bernard Sexton

Al - le - lu - ia, al - le - lu - ia, Al - le - lú - ia.

Al - le - lu - ia, al - le - lu - ia, al - le - lú - ia.

D.F.

Ghráigh Dia an domhan chomh mór sin
gur thug sé a Aonghin Mic   u-aidh i   dtreo

gach duine a chreideann ann, go mbeadh an bheatha   shío-raí   ai - ge.

Aifreann Eoin Na Croise

CD 2 / Track 73

Peadar ó Riada

Al-le-lu - ia, Al-le-lu - ia ó_ Al-le-lu - ia.

An bhea - tha shíor - aí, Al - le - lu - ia.

An bhea - tha shíor - aí, Al le - lu - ia.

Funerals

Mass Of Saint Finbarr

CD 2 / Track 74

Patrick Killeen

Al-le-lu-ia, Al - le - lu-ia, Al-le-lu-ia___ Al - le - lu-ia.

Tone 2

I am the resurrection and the life,   says   the   Lord:

those who believe in me, even though they die,   will___   live.

Funerals

Mass Of Saint Finbarr

CD 2 / Track 75

Patrick Killeen

Al - le - lu - ia, Al - le - lu - ia, Al - le - lu - ia___ Al - le - lu - ia.

Tone 2

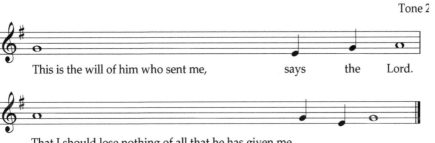

This is the will of him who sent me, says the Lord.

That I should lose nothing of all that he has given me,
but raise it up on the last day.

Funerals

Mass Of Saint Finbarr

CD 2 / Track 76

Patrick Killeen

Al - le - lu - ia, Al - le - lu - ia, Al - le - lu - ia___ Al - le - lu - ia.

Tone 2

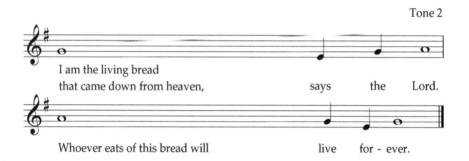

I am the living bread
that came down from heaven, says the Lord.

Whoever eats of this bread will live for - ever.

Mass Of The Annunciation

CD 2 / Track 77

Fintan O' Carroll

Al - le - lu - ia, al - le - lu - ia,

al - le - lu - ia, al - le - lu - ia.

D.F.

Come, you that are blessed by my Father, says the Lord;

inherit the kingdom prepared for you
from the foundation of the world.

Funerals

Mass Of The Annunciation

CD 2 / Track 78

Fintan O' Carroll

Al - le - lu - ia, al - le - lu - ia,
al - le - lu - ia, al - le - lu - ia.

D.F.

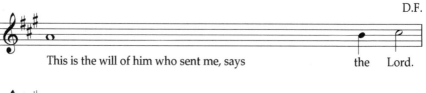

This is the will of him who sent me, says the Lord.

That I should lose nothing of all that he has given me,
but raise it up on the last day.

Funerals

CD 2 / Track 79 **Mass Of Saint John Of The Cross** R. McDonagh

Al - le-lu - ia, al - le - lu - ia, al - le - lu - ia.

D.F.

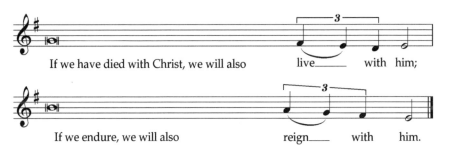

If we have died with Christ, we will also live____ with him;

If we endure, we will also reign____ with him.

Funerals

CD 2 / Track 80 # Mass Of Saint John Of The Cross R. McDonagh

Al - le-lu - ia, al - le - lu - ia, al - le-lu - ia.

D.F.

This is the will of him who sent me, says the Lord.

That I should lose nothing
of all that he has given me, but raise it up on the last day.

Mass Of Saint Finbarr

CD 2 / Track 81

Patrick Killeen

Al - le - lu - ia, Al - le - lu - ia, Al - le - lu - ia___ Al - le - lu - ia.

Tone 2

If you continue in my word, you are truly   my   dis - ciples;

and you will know the truth, and the truth will   make   you   free.

Saints

Mass Of The Annunciation

CD 2 / Track 82

Fintan O' Carroll

Al - le - lu - ia, al - le - lu - ia,

al - le - lu - ia, al - le - lu - ia.

D.F.

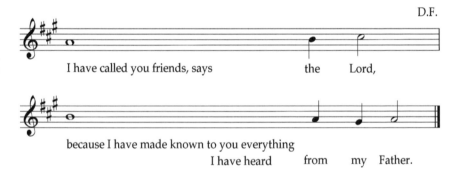

I have called you friends, says the Lord,

because I have made known to you everything
I have heard from my Father.

Mass Of Saint John Of The Cross

CD 2 / Track 83   R. McDonagh

Al - le-lu - ia, al - le - lu - ia, al - le - lu - ia.

D.F.

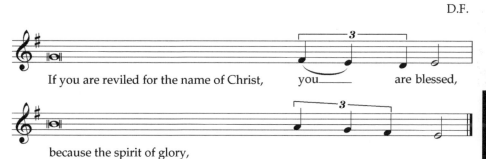

If you are reviled for the name of Christ, you____ are blessed,

because the spirit of glory,
which is the Spirit of God, is rest - ing on you.

Mass For The People

CD 2 / Track 84

Mary Pedder Daly

Al - le - lu - ia, al - le - lu - ia, al - le - lu - u - ia.

al - le - lu - ia, al - le - lu - ia, al - le - lu - ia.

Mary

Hail Mary, full of grace; the Lord is with you!

Blessed are you a - mong women.

Mass Of The Annunciation

CD 2 / Track 85

Fintan O' Carroll

Al - le - lu - ia, al - le - lu - ia,

al - le - lu - ia, al - le - lu - ia.

D.F.

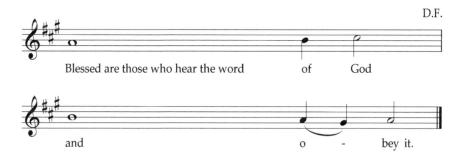

Blessed are those who hear the word of God

and o - bey it.

Mary

Mass Of The Annunciation

CD 2 / Track 86

Fintan O' Carroll

Al - le - lu - ia, al - le - lu - ia,

al - le - lu - ia, al - le - lu - ia.

D.F.

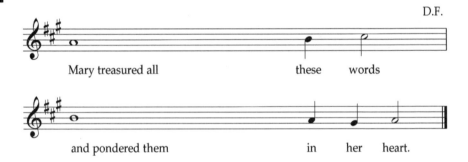

Mary treasured all these words

and pondered them in her heart.

CD 2 / Track 87 # Mass Of Saint John Of The Cross R. McDonagh

Al - le -lu - ia, al - le - lu - ia, al - le - lu - ia.

D.F.

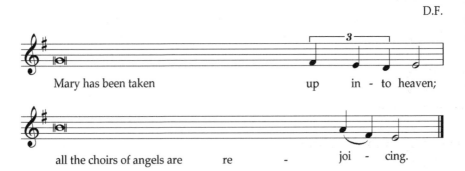

Mary has been taken up in - to heaven;

all the choirs of angels are re - joi - cing.

Mary

Extra Gospel Acclamation Texts - Not Recorded

◆ Saint Stephen, First Martyr
Mass Of Peace
Blessed is the one who comes in the <u>name</u> of the Lord.
The Lord is God, and he has given <u>us</u> light.

Mass Of Light
Blessed is the one who comes in the name of <u>the</u> Lord.
The Lord is God, and he has giv<u>en</u> us light.

◆ Saint John, Apostle and Evangelist
Mass Of Peace
We praise you, O God, we acknowledge you to <u>be</u> the Lord.
The glorious company of the apostles praise you, <u>O</u> Lord.

Mass Of Light
We praise you, O God, we acknowledge you to be <u>the</u> Lord.
The glorious company of the apostles praise <u>you,</u> O Lord.

◆ The Holy Innocents, Martyrs
Mass Of Peace
We praise you, O God, we acknowledge you to <u>be</u> the Lord.
The noble army of martyrs praise you, <u>O</u> Lord.

Mass Of Light
We praise you, O God, we acknowledge you to be <u>the</u> Lord.
The noble army of martyrs praise <u>you,</u> O Lord.

◆ The Epiphany of the Lord
Mass Of Peace
We observed his <u>star</u> at its rising,
and have come to pay <u>him</u> homage.

Mass Of Light
We observed his star at <u>its</u> rising,
and have come to <u>pay</u> him homage.

Extra Gospel Acclamation Texts - Not Recorded

First Sunday of Lent - A
Mass Of Creation –
One does not live by bread <u>a</u>lone,
but by every word that comes from the <u>mouth</u> of God.

Second Sunday of Lent - B
Mass Of Creation
From the cloud there came <u>a</u> voice,
'This is my Son, the Beloved; list<u>en</u> to him'!

Third Sunday of Lent - C
Mass Of Creation
I am the resurrection and the life, says <u>the</u> Lord:
those who believe in me, even though they <u>die</u>, will live.

Fourth Sunday of Lent - D
Mass Of Creation
God so loved the world that he gave his on<u>ly</u> Son,
so that everyone who believes in him may not perish
but may have <u>et</u>ernal life.

Fifth Sunday of Lent - E
Mass Of Creation –
I am the resurrection and the life, says <u>the</u> Lord:
those who believe in me, even though they <u>die</u>, will live.

Extra Gospel Acclamation Texts - Not Recorded

◆ **The Solemnity of the Annunciation of the Lord** [During the Season of Easter]
Paschal Mass
Alleluia
The Word became flesh and lived among us;
and we have seen his glory.

Mass Of God's Promise
Alleluia
The Word became flesh and lived among us;
and we have seen his glory.

Mode VI
Alleluia
The Word became flesh and lived among us;
and we have seen his glory.

◆ **Saints Philip and James, Apostles**
Paschal Mass
I am the way, and the truth, and the life, says the Lord.
Philip, whoever has seen me has seen the Father.

Mass Of God's Promise
I am the way, and the truth, and the life, says the Lord.
Philip, whoever has seen me has seen the Father.

Mode VI
I am the way, and the truth, and the life, says the Lord.
Philip, whoever has seen me has seen the Father.

Extra Gospel Acclamation Texts - Not Recorded

◆ **Saint Matthew, Apostle and Evangelist, Saint Simon and Jude, Apostles**
Mass Of Saint Finbarr
We praise you, O God, we acknowledge you to <u>be</u> the Lord.
The glorious company of the apostles praise <u>you</u>, O Lord.

Mass Of The Annunciation
We praise you, O God, we acknowledge you to be <u>the</u> Lord.
The glorious company of the apostles praise <u>you</u>, O Lord.

Mass Of Saint John Of The Cross
We praise you, O God, we acknowledge you to <u>be</u> the Lord.
The glorious company of the apostles praise <u>you</u>, O Lord.

◆ **Saint Andrew, Apostle**
Mass Of Saint Finbarr
Follow me, <u>says</u> the Lord,
and I will make you <u>fish</u> for people.

Mass Of The Annunciation
Follow me, says <u>the</u> Lord,
and I will make you <u>fish</u> for people.

Mass Of Saint John Of The Cross
Follow me, <u>says</u> the Lord,
and I will make you <u>fish</u> for people.

Extra Gospel Acclamation Texts - Not Recorded

◆ The Birthday of the Blessed Virgin Mary
Mass Of Saint Finbarr
Blessed are you, holy Virgin Mary,
and most worthy <u>of</u> all praise,
for the sun of justice, Christ our God,
was <u>born</u> of you.

Mass Of The Annunciation
Blessed are you, holy Virgin Mary,
and most worthy of <u>all</u> praise,
for the sun of justice, Christ our God,
was <u>born</u> of you.

Mass Of Saint John Of The Cross
Blessed are you, holy Virgin Mary,
and most worthy <u>of</u> all praise,
for the sun of justice, Christ our God,
was <u>born</u> of you.

Glossary

Alleluia: The most joyful word there is for praising God.
See: *The Ministry of the Word – A Compilation of Sources*, page 10.

Cantor: The minister who leads and sustains the singing of the liturgical assembly.
See: *The Ministry of the Word – A Compilation of Sources*, page 13.

Congregation: The members of the liturgical assembly, *excluding* the presider.
See: *The Ministry of the Word – A Compilation of Sources*, page 15.

Christian Initiation: The process by which Christians are made and sustained. It is marked by the celebration of the sacraments of Baptism, Confirmation and Eucharist.

Gospel Acclamation of the day: The Gospel acclamation text as assigned in the *Lectionary* to each day of the liturgical year. The Gospel acclamation rite is to be sung in celebrations with a congregation.
See: *The Ministry of the Word – A Compilation of Sources*, page 17

Lectionary: A major book of the Church that sets out the passages of Scripture which are proclaimed in the Liturgy. In Ireland, the *Lectionary* is published as three volumes.
See: *The Ministry of the Word – A Compilation of Sources*, pages 19-20.

(Liturgical) Assembly: The congregation *and* the presider. (The assembly is celebrant of the Liturgy).
See: *The Ministry of the Word – A Compilation of Sources*, page 12.

Liturgical Calendar for Ireland: An authoritative annual publication which identifies the liturgical season and day being celebrated. It cites the Scripture texts which the Church has assigned to each day. It states that presiders are not to set aside this schedule of Scripture needlessly or too often. It notes when certain ritual texts are not permitted. Personal copies can be purchased from Veritas. A reference copy is also kept in the church sacristy.
See: *The Ministry of the Word – A Compilation of Sources*, page 21.

Liturgical Day: As opposed to the civic calendar. For example, The First Sunday of Advent - not January 1st - is the first day of the Church's year. Also, while society can be in full swing celebrating "Christmas" by the First Sunday of Advent, the Church that day, instead, is undertaking four weeks of spiritual preparation for celebrating the liturgical days of Christmas, which occur from December 25th to circa January 6th.

Liturgical Law: The requirements and regulations for the legitimate and fruitful celebration of the Liturgy, as set down in the ritual books of the Church, in its Code of Canon Law and in its official decrees and documents.

Liturgical Season: i.e. any of the following, namely: Advent, Christmas, Ordinary Time, Lent, the Easter Triduum and Easter.
See: *The Ministry of the Word – A Compilation of Sources*, page 21.

Musical Setting: Music notation as applied to key texts of the Liturgy. Examples are: *Mass for the People, Mass of Saint Finbarr, Mass of Peace, Mass of Creation* and *Aifreann Eoin na Croise.*

Order of Christian Funerals: This is the series of funeral rites of the Roman Catholic Church. As well as the Funeral Mass, these rites also include: the 'Vigil for the Deceased'; the 'Reception of the Body at the Church', and the; 'Funeral Liturgy Outside Mass'.
See: *The Ministry of the Word – A Compilation of Sources*, Page 30.

Presider: The role which the priest-celebrant (or in his absence, the deacon or a deputed lay person) has in the liturgical assembly, in the course of celebrating the Liturgy.
See: *The Ministry of the Word – A Compilation of Sources*, Page 25.

Rite of Christian Initiation of Adults: The process by which the Church initiates adults and children of catechetical age. Adults and children of catechetical age who choose to become Christian participate in a process of Christian formation (i.e. the catechumenate), not unlike an apprenticeship. Then, on the First Sunday of Lent, after a liturgical year, at least, (or as long as it takes) of journeying with the parish in response to Christ, these catechumens are elected to celebrate Baptism, Confirmation and their First Eucharist during the forthcoming Easter Vigil.

Solemnity: A higher ranking feast.
See: *The Ministry of the Word – A Compilation of Sources*, Page 28.

Alphabetical List of Gospel Acclamation Texts

A light for revelation to the gentiles
and for glory to your people Israel.　　　　　　　　　　　　55

Be alert at all times, praying that you may have the strength
to stand before the Son of Man.　　　　　　　　　　　　150

Be faithful until death, says the Lord,
and I will give you the crown of life.　　　　　　　　　149

Bless the Lord, all his hosts, his ministers that do his will.　　　135, 136, 137

Blessed are the pure in heart, for they will see God.　　　　54

Blessed are those who hear the word of God and obey it.　　50, 126, 127, 128, 179

Blessed are you, holy Virgin Mary,
and most worthy of all praise,
for the sun of justice, Christ our God,
was born of you.　　　　　　　　　　　　　　　　186 (NR)

Blessed be God, a gentle Father and the God of all consolation,
who comforts us in all our sorrows.　　　　　　　　164

Blessed is she who believed that there would be a fulfillment
of what was spoken to her by the Lord.　　　　　　105

Blessed is the one who comes in the name of the Lord!
Blessed is the coming kingdom of our ancestor David!　　151, 152, 153

Blessed is the one who comes in the name of the Lord.
The Lord is God, and he has given us light.　　　　182 (NR)

Alphabetical List of Gospel Acclamation Texts

Christ humbled himself
and became obedient to the point of death,
even death on a cross.
Therefore, God also highly exalted him
and gave him the name
that is above every other name.   64, 68, 165

Come, Holy Spirit, fill the hearts of your faithful
and kindle in them the fire of your love.   75, 78, 81, 87, 88, 89

Come to me, all you that are weary
and are carrying heavy burdens, and I will give you rest.   139, 140, 141

Come you nations, worship the Lord,
for today a great light has shone down upon the earth.   30

'Come, you that are blessed by my Father, says the Lord;
inherit the kingdom prepared for you
from the foundation of the world.   171

Create in me a clean heart, O God,
restore to me the joy of your salvation.   57, 159

Follow me, says the Lord,
and I will make you fish for people.   185 (NR)

From the cloud there came a voice,
'This is my Son, the Beloved; listen to him'!   33, 37, 183 (NR)

Glory be to the Father, and to the Son, and to the Holy Spirit,
the God who is and who was, and who is to come.   106, 107, 108

Alphabetical List of Gospel Acclamation Texts

God is love, and those who abide in love abide in God,
and God abides in them.   156

God is love; since God loved us so much,
we also, ought to love one another.   154

God so loved the world that he gave his only Son,
so that everyone who believes in him may not perish
but may have eternal life.   183 (NR)

Go into all the world, says the Lord,
and proclaim the good news to the whole creation.   83

Go, therefore, make disciples of all nations.
I am with you always to the end of the age.   74, 77, 80

Hail, Mary, full of grace; the Lord is with you!
Blessed are you among women.   25, 28, 178

Hail to you, our King!
You alone have had compassion on our sins.   65

Happy are those who live in your house,
ever singing your praise.   62

Have you believed because you have seen me?
Blessed are those who have not seen
and yet have come to believe.   113

Alphabetical List of Gospel Acclamation Texts

He came as a witness to testify to the light,
to make ready a people prepared for the Lord.   116, 117, 118

I am the good shepherd, says the Lord;
I know my own and my own know me.   112

I am the light of the world, says the Lord;
whoever follows me will have the light of life.   51, 99

I am the living bread that came down from heaven,
says the Lord. Whoever eats of this bread will live forever.
                                    90, 93, 94, 109, 110, 111, 170

I am the resurrection and the life, says the Lord:
those who believe in me, even though they die,
will live.   168, 183 (NR)

I am the way, and the truth, and the life, says the Lord.
No one comes to the Father except through me.   84

I am the way, and the truth, and the life, says the Lord.
Philip, whoever has seen me has seen the Father.   184 (NR)

I chose you.
And I appointed you to go and bear fruit,
fruit that will last, says the Lord.   53

I have called you friends, says the Lord,
because I have made known to you
everything I have heard from my Father.   138, 176

Alphabetical List of Gospel Acclamation Texts

I have chosen and consecrated this house, says the Lord,
so that my name may be there for ever.   145, 146, 147

If you are reviled for the name of Christ, you are blessed,
because the spirit of glory, which is the Spirit of God,
is resting on you.   124, 177

If you continue in my word, you are truly my disciples;
and you will know the truth, and the truth will make you free.   91, 122, 175

If we have died with Christ, we will also live with him;
if we endure, we will also reign with him.   173

If we love one another;
God lives in us, and his love is perfected in us   155

I give you a new commandment:
that you love one another.   67

I have called you friends, says the Lord,
because I have made known to you
everything I have heard from my Father.   123

Jesus Christ, the faithful witness,
the firstborn of the dead
and the ruler of the kings of the earth;
you have made us to be a kingdom,
priests serving his God and Father.   86

Let the peace of Christ rule in your hearts;
let the word of Christ dwell in you.   31, 162

Alphabetical List of Gospel Acclamation Texts

Look, the Lord will come to save his people.
Blessed those who are ready to meet him. 24, 16

Lord, you know everything; you know that I love you. 119, 120, 12
Make me know your ways, O Lord;
lead me in your truth. 95, 16

Make me understand the way of your precepts
and I will meditate on your wondrous works. 10

Mary has been taken up into heaven;
all the choirs of angels are rejoicing. 129, 130, 131, 18

Mary treasured all these words
and pondered them in her heart. 18

Morning star, radiance of eternal light, sun of justice,
come and enlighten those who live in darkness
and in the shadow of death. 2

Most Reverend Father, I bring you a message of great joy,
the message of Alleluia. 6

O Come, you nations, worship the Lord,
for today a great light has shone down upon the earth. 3

One does not live by bread alone,
but by every word that comes from the mouth of God. 101, 183 (NR)

Alphabetical List of Gospel Acclamation Texts

Our paschal lamb, Christ, has been sacrificed;
let us celebrate the festival then, in the Lord. 72

Our savior, Christ Jesus, who abolished death
has brought life and immortality to light
through the gospel. 85

Prepare the way of the Lord, make his paths straight.
And all flesh shall see the salvation of God. 27

See, now is the acceptable time;
see, now is the day of salvation. 58

Speak, Lord, for your servant is listening:
You have the words of eternal life. 97

Stand up and raise your heads,
because your redemption is drawing near. 148

The Lord has sent me with Good News;
the wonder of salvation.
Proclaiming justice, love and truth.
Go forth to every nation. 104

The people who sat in darkness have seen a great light,
and for those who sat in the region and shadow of death,
light has dawned. 36, 163

The Spirit of the Lord God is upon me.
He has anointed me to bring good news to the poor. 66

Alphabetical List of Gospel Acclamation Texts

The Spirit of the Lord has anointed me
to bring good news to the poor.
He has sent me to proclaim release to captives.   32, 56

The Word became flesh and lived among us;
and we have seen his glory.   63, 184 (NR)

The Word became flesh and lived among us.
To all who received him, he gave power to become
children of God.   34

The Word of God is living and active;
it is able to judge the thoughts and intentions
of the heart.   103

"This is my Son, the Beloved;
with him I am well pleased; listen to him"!   125

This is the will of him who sent me, says the Lord.
That I should lose nothing of all that he has given me,
but raise it up on the last day.   142, 143, 144, 169, 172, 174

Those who love me will keep my word,
says the Lord,
and my Father will love them,
and we will come to them.   98

We adore you, O Christ, and we bless you;
because by your cross you have redeemed the world.   132, 133, 134

Alphabetical List of Gospel Acclamation Texts

We know that Christ is truly risen from the dead;
have mercy on us, triumphant King. 73, 76, 79

We observed his star at its rising,
and have come to pay him homage. 182 (NR)

We praise you, O God, we acknowledge you to be the Lord.
The glorious company of the apostles praise you, O Lord. 182 (NR), 185(NR)

We praise you, O God, we acknowledge you to be the Lord.
The noble army of martyrs praise you, O Lord. 182 (NR)

We proclaim Christ crucified.
Christ the power of God and the wisdom of God. 114

Welcome with meekness the implanted word
that has the power to save your souls. 96

Wisdom of the Most High,
ordering all things with strength and gentleness,
come and teach us the way of truth. 29

You are a chosen race, a royal priesthood, a holy nation,
God's own people.
Proclaim the mighty acts of him
who called you out of darkness
into his marvelous light. 82, 92

You are Peter, and on this rock I will build my church,
and the gates of Hades will not prevail against it. 52, 61

Alphabetical List of Gospel Acclamation Texts

You did not choose me, but I chose you,
and I appointed you to go and bear fruit,
fruit that will last.   115

You shine like stars in the world
by your holding fast to the word of life.   100

Alphabetical List of Gospel Acclamation Texts
Irish Language

An bheatha shíoraí, Alleluia.
An bheatha shíoraí, Alleluia.   167

Chuir an Tiarna uaidh mé ag tabhairt an Dea-Scéil
do na bochta ag fógairt a scaoilte do bhraighde. Alleluia/Glóir duit...   43, 59

Dea-Scéil do na bochta, Alleluia
Dea-Scéil do na bochta, Alleluia   49

Ghráigh Dia an domhan chomh mór sin
gur thug sé a Aonghin Mic uaidh i dtreo,
Gach duine a chreideann ann,
go mbeadh an bheatha shíoraí aige.   166

Glan ó chroí, Alleluia.
Glan ó chroí, Alleluia.   47

Glóir duit, a Chríost, is tú briathar Dé!
Chuir an Tiarna uaidh mé ag tabhairt an Dea-Scéil
do na bochta
ag fógairt a scaoilte do bhraighde.   59

Glóir do phobail, Alleluia.
Glóir do phobail, Alleluia.   48

'Is mise solas an t-saoil' a deir an Tiarna.
'An té a leanfaidh mise, beidh aige solas na beatha'.   38

Is tú Peadar, agus is ar an gcarraig seo a thógfaidh mé m'Eaglais,
agus ní bhuafaidh geataí ifrinn uirthi.   39

Alphabetical List of Gospel Acclamation Texts
Irish Language

Is tú Peadar, Alleluia.
Is tú Peadar, Alleluia.   45

Le guth an Tiarna, Alleluia.
Le guth an Tiarna, Alleluia.   44

Maireann Dia ionainn, Alleluia.
Maireann Dia ionainn, Alleluia.   158

Mairfead bhur dtoradh, Alleluia.
Mairfead bhur dtoradh, Alleluia.   46

Má thugaimid grá dá cheile,
maireann Dia ionainn
agus is lánfhoirfe ionainn a ghrá.   157

Moladh duit, a Chríost, rí na glóire síoraí,
Ó moladh duit, a Chríost.
Dea-Scéil do na bochta, moladh duit, a Chríost.
Dea-Scéil do na bochta, moladh duit, a Chríost.   60

Rinne mé sibh a thoghagh,
agus a cheapadh chun go n-imeodh sibh
agus toradh a thabhairt agus go mairfead bhur dtoradh.   40

Solas chun na náisiúin a shoilsiú agus glóir do phobail, Isráél.   42

Tar, a chéile Chríost;
glac an choróin atá ullamh ag Críost duit ón tsíoraíocht i leith.   41

Index of Musical Settings

Index of Musical Settings